Cambridge School
Shakespeare

D0289171

Julius Caesar

Edited by Rob Smith

Series Editor: Rex Gibson
Director, Shakespeare and Schools Project

Series Editorial Group: Richard Andrews, Mike Clamp, Perry Mills, Rob Smith

CAMBRIDGE
UNIVERSITY PRESS

CAMBRIDGE UNIVERSITY PRESS
Cambridge, New York, Melbourne, Madrid, Cape Town, Singapore, São Paulo, Delhi

Cambridge University Press
The Edinburgh Building, Cambridge CB2 8RU, UK

www.cambridge.org
Information on this title: www.cambridge.org/9780521706773

First published 2008

Printed in the United Kingdom at the University Press, Cambridge

A catalogue record for this publication is available from the British Library

ISBN   978-0-521-70677-3 paperback

ACKNOWLEDGEMENTS
Thanks are due to the following for permission to reproduce illustrations:
Cover, v, vi, vii, viii, ix, x, xi, xii, 5, 6, 14, 34, 39, 40, 56, 62, 73, 74, 76, 80, 96, 98,
111, 139, 165, 175, 177, 179, 181, 183, 190, 193, 194, Donald Cooper/Photostage;
52, © British Library Board, all rights reserved, C.57.L.2; 108, Reg Wilson; 109, 122,
© copyright the Trustees of the British Museum.

Cover design by Smith

Contents

List of characters   1

Before the play begins   2

Julius Caesar   7

What is the play about?   166

The Roman world   171

Characters   174

The language of *Julius Caesar*   184

Julius Caesar in performance   190

William Shakespeare   196

Cambridge School
Shakespeare

This edition of *Julius Caesar* is part of the **Cambridge School Shakespeare** series. Like every other play in the series, it has been specially prepared to help all students in schools and colleges.

This *Julius Caesar* aims to be different from other editions of the play. It invites you to bring the play to life in your classroom, hall or drama studio through enjoyable activities that will increase your understanding. Actors have created their different interpretations of the play over the centuries. Similarly, you are encouraged to make up your own mind about *Julius Caesar*, rather than having someone else's interpretation handed down to you.

Cambridge School Shakespeare does not offer you a cut-down or simplified version of the play. This is Shakespeare's language, filled with imaginative possibilities. You will find on every left-hand page: a summary of the action, an explanation of unfamiliar words, a choice of activities on Shakespeare's language, characters and stories.

Between each act and in the pages at the end of the play, you will find notes, illustrations and activities. These will help to increase your understanding of the whole play.

There are a large number of activities to give you the widest choice to suit your own particular needs. Please don't think you have to do every one. Choose the activities that will help you most.

This edition will be of value to you whether you are studying for an examination, reading for pleasure, or thinking of putting on the play to entertain others. You can work on the activities on your own or in groups. Many of the activities suggest a particular group size, but don't be afraid to make up larger or smaller groups to suit your own purposes.

Although you are invited to treat *Julius Caesar* as a play, you don't need special dramatic or theatrical skills to do the activities. By choosing your activities, and by exploring and experimenting, you can make your own interpretations of Shakespeare's language, characters and stories. Whatever you do, remember that Shakespeare wrote his plays to be acted, watched and enjoyed.

Rex Gibson

This edition of *Julius Caesar* uses the text of the play established by Marvin Spevack in **The New Cambridge Shakespeare**.

iv

Beware the Ides of March: Shakespeare's play dramatises the political machinations surrounding the assassination of Julius Caesar. The action is focused around three characters: Mark Antony (left), Julius Caesar (centre) and Marcus Brutus (right).

There has been a terrible civil war. Pompey and Caesar – both formidable figures of the Roman Empire – have fought each other for supreme power in Rome, and Caesar has won. The play opens with the tradespeople of Rome celebrating Caesar's victory.

Marcus Brutus is Caesar's close friend and military comrade. His ancestors were famed for driving the tyrannical King Tarquin from the throne and helping to found the Roman Republic.

A group of conspirators, envious of Caesar's increasing power, grow restless in Rome. They are initially led by Cassius (far right).

Brutus (left) becomes convinced that Caesar is greedy for power, and intends to turn republican Rome into a monarchy. He decides that Caesar must die for his ambition to be king, and agrees to assist in the assassination attempt planned by the conspiring senators.

Brutus' wife, Portia, grows fearful for his health and suspects Brutus of deviousness.

Meanwhile, Caesar's wife, Calpurnia, has spoken of his murder in her sleep. She orders him to stay at home, telling of frightening and ominous portents. But Caesar is unmoved.

Et tu, Brute? Ignoring the Soothsayer's and his wife's premonitions, Caesar resolves to go to the Senate and is caught at the mercy of the conspirators. Having declared himself the world's only constant man, he is stabbed to death. His friend Brutus' betrayal shocks him profoundly.

Friends, Romans, countrymen, lend me your ears. Following Caesar's death, his friend Mark Antony delivers an eloquent and rousing speech over Caesar's corpse. He deftly turns public opinion against the assassins. The common people drive the conspirators from Rome.

Caesar's great-nephew, Octavius, arrives in Rome and forms the Triumvirate with Antony and Lepidus. Antony and Octavius (standing, centre) decide to go to war against Brutus (seated right) and Cassius (left).

Brutus (left) berates Cassius for corruptly and dishonourably accepting bribes. He is also distressed by the news of his wife's death. Brutus and Cassius are reconciled but, as they prepare for war, Caesar's ghost appears to Brutus with a warning of defeat.

Events go badly for the conspirators during the battle. Both Cassius and Brutus (the latter pictured here with his slave Strato) choose to commit suicide rather than be captured.

The play ends with Antony's tribute to Brutus, who has remained 'the noblest Roman of them all', and hints at the friction between Mark Antony and Octavius that will characterise another of Shakespeare's plays, *Antony and Cleopatra*.

List of characters

Caesar and his supporters

JULIUS CAESAR
CALPURNIA   his wife
MARK ANTONY   ⎫
OCTAVIUS CAESAR   ⎬ The ruling Triumvirate after Caesar's death
LEPIDUS   ⎭

The conspirators against Caesar

Conspirators

BRUTUS   CASCA   CINNA   METELLUS CIMBER

CAIUS CASSIUS   DECIUS BRUTUS   TREBONIUS   CAIUS LIGARIUS

Family and followers

PORTIA   Brutus' wife
LUCIUS   Brutus' boy servant
CLAUDIO   ⎫
LABEO*   ⎪
FLAVIUS*   ⎬ Personal followers of Brutus
CLITUS   ⎪
STRATO   ⎪
DARDANIUS   ⎭

VARRUS
PINDARUS   Cassius' slave
LUCILIUS   ⎫
TITINIUS   ⎪
MESSALA   ⎬ Officers of Brutus and Cassius
YOUNG CATO   ⎪
VOLUMNIUS   ⎪
STATILIUS*   ⎭

Other Romans

CICERO   ⎫
PUBLIUS CIMBER   ⎬ Senators
POPILLIUS LENA   ⎪
OTHER SENATORS*   ⎭
FLAVIUS   ⎫ Tribunes critical of Caesar
MURELLUS   ⎭
SOOTHSAYER   ⎫ Who try to warn Caesar
ARTEMIDORUS   ⎭
SERVANTS TO CAESAR, ANTONY AND OCTAVIUS

CINNA THE POET
A CYNIC POET
1ST, 2ND, 3RD, 4TH PLEBEIANS
CARPENTER
COBBLER
MESSENGER

1ST, 2ND, 3RD SOLDIERS

OTHER PLEBEIANS*

* non-speaking parts

Before the play begins

When the Roman Senate granted Julius Caesar the title of dictator of Rome for life, it effectively signalled the end of the Roman Republic which had governed the city and its territories for more than four hundred years. The Republic had been founded when the inhabitants of Rome drove out the tyrannical Tarquin kings and set up their own form of government, in which they could elect their own leaders rather than being ruled by hereditary kings. At first, control of the Republic was entirely in the hands of the patricians, Rome's aristocratic class. Only patricians could be elected members of the Senate, or parliament, and only patricians could be chosen as heads of state, or consuls. To prevent any one man obtaining too much power, there were always two consuls elected at any one time, who could rule for one year only. Consuls were primarily military commanders who would lead Rome's armies in war. In times of great emergency a dictator (supreme commander) was appointed in place of the consuls, but for a period of no more than six months.

In time the plebeians, the ordinary citizens of Rome, campaigned for and achieved the right to have their say in how they were to be ruled. They were allowed to elect two tribunes to represent them in government and protect their interests. Eventually the plebeians gained their own assembly, and the right to propose laws and to require one of the two consuls to be chosen from their own class. But despite these concessions, the patricians still retained overall control of government, while the plebeians – who were far greater in number than the patricians – remained poor, discontented and ready to riot.

As the centuries passed the Roman Republic secured control of the rest of Italy, then Greece, Spain and North Africa, until it had conquered most of the countries surrounding the Mediterranean Sea. But as Rome's wealth increased, so the quality of its ruling classes declined. The patrician class became more interested in luxurious living than in public service, and power gradually gravitated into the hands of a few men who could use their wealth and private armies to control the power of the Senate and eliminate their political enemies.

Two such great rivals were Caesar and Pompey. Although for a while it suited the two men to form an uneasy political alliance, it was inevitable that they would eventually come to blows. In the bitter civil war which followed, Pompey was defeated and fled to Egypt, where he was murdered. In 48 BC the Senate created Caesar *dictator perpetuus* (i.e. made him permanent head of government) and granted him many other powers and honours. There was even a statue of him placed in one of the Roman temples with the inscription 'To the Unconquerable God'. Caesar was now sole ruler of Rome and its Empire. He was king in all but name.

Caesar was, however, surprisingly merciful to most of his defeated Roman opponents (including Brutus and Cassius) and gave a number of them responsible positions in his new regime. But the great unanswered question was how he would use his supreme power over the government of the Republic. Would he use it to reform and strengthen the old republican system which had so clearly failed to maintain control of Rome's vast Empire? Or did he intend to establish a new monarchy with himself as the first king or emperor?

Some of the patricians were genuinely fearful that Caesar secretly intended to return Rome to monarchical rule. One such was Marcus Brutus, once a supporter of Pompey but now a close friend of Caesar. Brutus was a committed Republican and boasted a distinguished ancestor who had helped expel the Tarquin kings and establish the original Republic. Some patricians became so desperate that in 44 BC they formed a secret conspiracy to assassinate Caesar before he could make himself king. One of its leaders was Caius Cassius, another former supporter of Pompey in the recent civil war.

This is the point at which Shakespeare begins his story. The figure of Julius Caesar held a particular fascination for the Elizabethans. Some admired his military skill, strong leadership and generous treatment of former enemies. Others condemned him for his ruthlessness, for his weakening of the powers of the Senate and above all for his ambition.

The Elizabethans were also divided in their attitude to the conspirators. If some felt Caesar's murder was justified to help preserve the Republic, others believed it to be a wicked act, or at the very least a major political misjudgement resulting in the very thing the conspirators were trying to prevent: the collapse of Rome's republican governmental system. Brutus in particular enjoyed a double reputation. He was seen as an honest man of principle and a champion of liberty. Yet by joining the conspiracy he became also the man who treacherously murdered his friend and benefactor.

Whatever the Elizabethans may or may not have thought of Caesar and the rights or wrongs of his assassination, fewer than fifty years after Shakespeare wrote his play the English people executed their own king and set up their own republican form of government under Oliver Cromwell.

Pompey and the Senate! Caesar and the people!
(in groups A and B of four or five each)

There has been a terrible civil war. Pompey and Caesar – heroes always named in one breath – have fought each other for supreme power in Rome, and Caesar has won.

All of you are Romans after the war. Group A supports Pompey, who wants to rule more democratically, through the elected assembly of the Senate. Group B supports Caesar, who wants the direct personal rule of a dictator.

A A Pompeyite's point of view

'Pompey believed in the Senate. He fought for the Senate, he died for the Senate. One-person rule is dangerous – who's to stop Caesar becoming a tyrant? One ruler may serve us well, but what will happen when that person dies? Do we want all that superstitious nonsense about monarchs? We killed the last king we had four hundred years ago!'

Make a list of the benefits of senatorial rule as you see it, at a time when there was no education for ordinary people.

B A Caesarite's point of view

'People in Rome are poor. Only the rich get votes in the Senate. Yes, the rich look after themselves. But with Caesar, you ask and you get. He listens and then he takes action – and he's richer than the Senate, because he's been off on his conquests again. Let him rule! Let him be a dictator! We need a strong man after the wars. But we'll never let him be king, of course.'

Make a list of the benefits of one-person rule as you see it, at a time when there was no education for ordinary people.

When you have made your lists, set out for Caesar's Triumph. You want to prevent it and make trouble, or to cheer and enjoy yourselves. Improvise what happens when Pompeyites and Caesarites meet.

Caesar's Triumph!

1 Planning for a day at the Triumph (in groups of five)

Your family get ready for a day on the streets: packed lunch, cagoules, children to be prepared. Everyone is talking all the time about what they've heard and what they will see. Discuss together what needs to be done before you set out, and make a detailed list in the right order.

2 At the Triumph (whole class)

You arrived late. You are all at the back of the crowd. But you, as children, may climb up high (on tables and chairs) and talk about everything that is to be seen. Join in the cheering and shouting with everyone else. Welcome the victorious Caesar back to Rome!

Two Tribunes, Flavius and Murellus, ask some tradespeople why they are taking the day off. A Cobbler gives riddling replies.

1 Tribunes versus common people (in groups of four)

Poster for Royal Shakespeare Company production in 1983.

The opening of the play immediately establishes a sense of conflict. The Tribunes Flavius and Murellus (officials of the Roman government) are loyal to the defeated Pompey. They are angry that the common people celebrate Caesar's triumph in carnival mood. The Cobbler (which can also mean a person who plays with words) responds to the Tribunes' wrath with witty wordplay at their expense.

- Take the parts of Flavius, Murellus, the Cobbler and the Carpenter, and read lines 1–30 together. Experiment with different ways of bringing out the Tribunes' disapproval and the common people's celebration.
- Which line do you think is being spoken in the picture above?

mechanical manual workers, craftsmen
rule measuring ruler
apparel clothes
in respect of compared to
directly clearly, plainly

soles (a pun on 'souls')
naughty worthless
be not out don't be angry
if you be out if you (your shoes) are worn out

6

Julius Caesar

Act 1 Scene 1
Rome A street

Enter FLAVIUS, MURELLUS, and certain COMMONERS over the stage

FLAVIUS Hence! Home, you idle creatures, get you home!
    Is this a holiday? What, know you not,
    Being mechanical, you ought not walk
    Upon a labouring day without the sign
    Of your profession? Speak, what trade art thou?   5
CARPENTER Why, sir, a carpenter.
MURELLUS Where is thy leather apron and thy rule?
    What dost thou with thy best apparel on?
    You, sir, what trade are you?
COBBLER Truly, sir, in respect of a fine workman, I am but, as you would   10
    say, a cobbler.
MURELLUS But what trade art thou? Answer me directly.
COBBLER A trade, sir, that I hope I may use with a safe conscience, which
    is indeed, sir, a mender of bad soles.
FLAVIUS What trade, thou knave? Thou naughty knave, what trade?   15
COBBLER Nay, I beseech you, sir, be not out with me; yet if you be out, sir,
    I can mend you.
MURELLUS What mean'st thou by that? Mend me, thou saucy fellow?
COBBLER Why, sir, cobble you.
FLAVIUS Thou art a cobbler, art thou?   20

The tradespeople celebrate Caesar's triumph over Pompey. The Tribunes accuse them of ingratitude to Pompey, who was once the people's favourite.

---

1 Rhetorical questions (in groups of four or five)

Murellus' lines 31–50 make much use of rhetorical questions (questions that imply but do not demand an answer). They are intended to influence the thoughts of the listeners and make them reflect on their actions. Share the lines out, making sure everyone has at least one rhetorical question. Practise speaking them, deciding where to speak harshly, where softly. Surround another group and deliver the lines. Then they do the same to your group.

- Talk together about the effect the lines have on the listeners.
- As you read on, keep a note of how many times rhetorical questions are used as a device to persuade a listening audience.

2 The power of Roman superstition (in groups of three)

Ordinary Romans were deeply superstitious. Every action or decision was taken after consultation with the augurers, who performed rites and sacrifices to find out the will of the gods. They were immensely powerful priests.

Deliver lines 52–9 as if you were magicians or priests with power over the people. Try different ways of speaking, and decide which one would have the most effect on the common people.

3 How do the common people react? (in pairs)

The common people exit at line 59 – but Shakespeare gives no clue as to their mood. After listening to Murellus' chastening words are they subdued, resentful, angry or . . . what? Talk together about your ideas.

---

awl tool for piercing leather
neat's leather cattle hide
tributaries conquered peoples forced to pay tax
Pompey a great Roman general (see p. 173)

Tiber river, sacred to Romans, that flows through Rome
replication echo
cull out pick, choose
intermit prevent
Do kiss . . . of all rises to the top of its banks

COBBLER Truly, sir, all that I live by is with the awl. I meddle with no
tradesman's matters, nor women's matters; but withal I am indeed,
sir, a surgeon to old shoes: when they are in great danger I recover
them. As proper men as ever trod upon neat's leather have gone upon
my handiwork.   25

FLAVIUS But wherefore art not in thy shop today?
Why dost thou lead these men about the streets?

COBBLER Truly, sir, to wear out their shoes, to get myself into more work.
But indeed, sir, we make holiday to see Caesar and to rejoice in his
triumph.   30

MURELLUS Wherefore rejoice? What conquest brings he home?
What tributaries follow him to Rome
To grace in captive bonds his chariot wheels?
You blocks, you stones, you worse than senseless things!
O you hard hearts, you cruel men of Rome,   35
Knew you not Pompey? Many a time and oft
Have you climbed up to walls and battlements,
To towers and windows, yea, to chimney tops,
Your infants in your arms, and there have sat
The livelong day, with patient expectation,   40
To see great Pompey pass the streets of Rome.
And when you saw his chariot but appear
Have you not made an universal shout,
That Tiber trembled underneath her banks
To hear the replication of your sounds   45
Made in her concave shores?
And do you now put on your best attire?
And do you now cull out a holiday?
And do you now strew flowers in his way,
That comes in triumph over Pompey's blood?   50
Be gone!
Run to your houses, fall upon your knees,
Pray to the gods to intermit the plague
That needs must light on this ingratitude.

FLAVIUS Go, go, good countrymen, and for this fault   55
Assemble all the poor men of your sort,
Draw them to Tiber banks, and weep your tears
Into the channel till the lowest stream
Do kiss the most exalted shores of all.

Exeunt all the Commoners

The Tribunes leave, intending to stop further celebration. Caesar comes to the Lupercal races, in which Antony is to run. He orders Antony to touch Calpurnia in the race to cure her infertility.

1 First impressions of Caesar (in groups of three)

Caesar does not appear in Scene 1. But the loyal Pompeyite Flavius makes clear in lines 67–8 that he plans to take all the decorations off Caesar's statues. He is also anxious that Caesar should not be allowed to 'soar above the view of men / And keep us all in servile fearfulness'. Talk together about the picture of Caesar created by these details at this point in the play.

2 Murellus and Flavius reflect on events

Murellus and Flavius do not speak again in the play . . . but you can give them a voice. Improvise the dialogue they might have with each other about their meeting with the common people. How would they elaborate on their feelings about Pompey and Caesar?

3 Caesar's triumphal progress (in groups of six to eight)

Plan how Caesar's entrance and exit (lines 1–24) can be staged. A galaxy of decisions awaits you. How will you manage the Tribunes' exit at the end of the previous scene (to follow Caesar back on stage shortly afterwards)? How will you enact the stage direction at the start of this scene? What is the behaviour of the 'great crowd'? How do the different characters speak to, and about, Caesar? How does Caesar address his wife and how sensitive is he about her childlessness? What sort of person is the Soothsayer? How will you use music in the scene? (Consider Caesar's remark at line 16 and the 'Sennet' stage direction at line 24.)

Make your choices, then present your version of lines 1–24.

---

basest metal   inferior natures (with wordplay on metal/mettle; lead, the basest metal, is inert but malleable)
Capitol   Senate house or government building
Disrobe the images   pull decorations off the statues

feast of Lupercal   festival held on 15 February (see **The Lupercal**, p. 172)
Stand you directly . . . barren . . . sterile curse   a runner's touch was said to cure infertile women

See where their basest metal be not moved: 60
They vanish tongue-tied in their guiltiness.
Go you down that way towards the Capitol,
This way will I. Disrobe the images
If you do find them decked with ceremonies.
MURELLUS May we do so?   65
      You know it is the feast of Lupercal.
FLAVIUS It is no matter; let no images
      Be hung with Caesar's trophies. I'll about
      And drive away the vulgar from the streets;
      So do you too, where you perceive them thick.   70
      These growing feathers plucked from Caesar's wing
      Will make him fly an ordinary pitch,
      Who else would soar above the view of men
      And keep us all in servile fearfulness.

Exeunt

Act 1 Scene 2
Rome A street

Enter CAESAR, ANTONY for the course, CALPURNIA, Portia,
Decius, Cicero, BRUTUS, CASSIUS, CASCA, a SOOTHSAYER,
[a great crowd following]; after them Murellus and Flavius

CAESAR Calpurnia.
CASCA   Peace ho, Caesar speaks.
CAESAR   Calpurnia.
CALPURNIA Here, my lord.
CAESAR Stand you directly in Antonio's way
      When he doth run his course. Antonio.
ANTONY Caesar, my lord.   5
CAESAR Forget not in your speed, Antonio,
      To touch Calpurnia, for our elders say
      The barren, touchèd in this holy chase,
      Shake off their sterile curse.
ANTONY   I shall remember:
      When Caesar says, 'Do this', it is performed.   10

Caesar is warned to beware the Ides of March. He dismisses the warning, then leaves. Cassius remains with Brutus and accuses him of being unfriendly, but Brutus says he is troubled by private problems.

1 A break in the progress of Caesar (in groups of three or four)

Shakespeare wrote most of his plays in blank verse – lines of ten syllables. Though shared between the Soothsayer and Caesar, line 18 is a regular blank verse line of ten syllables. Count them, then count the syllables of other lines chosen at random.

Line 23 has only six syllables. These breaks often occur at moments of crucial importance. Shakespeare's actor must pause for four syllables (two 'beats') to think, to listen or to take action. How will Caesar, all eyes on him, play this moment of silence? The Ides, the fifteenth day of the month, are during the full moon, an unlucky time. No Roman will do business under the waning moon that follows. Today is the Ides of February, so the Ides of March are a month away.

From 'What man', play lines 18–24, taking it in turns to be Caesar. Think yourself into his mind at this moment. When you come to the pause at line 23, hold a thought of Caesar's in your head that the others must try to guess.

2 Brutus' troubles (in pairs)

With Caesar's exit the focus shifts to Cassius and Brutus. Cassius has noticed a cooling in their friendship, and Brutus confesses that he is 'with himself at war'. Again Shakespeare uses shortened lines (26, 27) to allow the two men to pause reflectively at the start of their discussion.

Take parts and read lines 25–47. Afterwards, discuss together the ways in which Brutus' character seems to have changed. As the scene further unfolds, write down in your own words exactly what *is* bothering him and why.

---

press   crowd
Ides of March   15 March
Sennet   formal, stately music played
  on wooden cornetts
gamesome   fond of sports and frivolity

You bear . . . Over   You are too cold
  and almost hostile to
soil   discredit
construe   interpret

CAESAR Set on, and leave no ceremony out.

SOOTHSAYER Caesar!

CAESAR Ha? Who calls?

CASCA Bid every noise be still – peace yet again!

CAESAR Who is it in the press that calls on me?   15
        I hear a tongue shriller than all the music
        Cry 'Caesar!' Speak, Caesar is turned to hear.

SOOTHSAYER Beware the Ides of March.

CAESAR   What man is that?

BRUTUS A soothsayer bids you beware the Ides of March.

CAESAR Set him before me, let me see his face.   20

CASSIUS Fellow, come from the throng, look upon Caesar.

CAESAR What say'st thou to me now? Speak once again.

SOOTHSAYER Beware the Ides of March.

CAESAR He is a dreamer, let us leave him. Pass.

                Sennet. Exeunt [all but] Brutus and Cassius

CASSIUS Will you go see the order of the course?   25

BRUTUS Not I.

CASSIUS I pray you, do.

BRUTUS I am not gamesome: I do lack some part
        Of that quick spirit that is in Antony.
        Let me not hinder, Cassius, your desires;   30
        I'll leave you.

CASSIUS Brutus, I do observe you now of late:
        I have not from your eyes that gentleness
        And show of love as I was wont to have.
        You bear too stubborn and too strange a hand   35
        Over your friend that loves you.

BRUTUS   Cassius,
        Be not deceived. If I have veiled my look
        I turn the trouble of my countenance
        Merely upon myself. Vexèd I am
        Of late with passions of some difference,   40
        Conceptions only proper to myself,
        Which give some soil, perhaps, to my behaviours.
        But let not therefore my good friends be grieved
        (Among which number, Cassius, be you one)
        Nor construe any further my neglect   45
        Than that poor Brutus, with himself at war,
        Forgets the shows of love to other men.

Cassius claims to help Brutus understand himself and the state of Rome.
Offstage the crowd shouts. Brutus fears they want Caesar crowned.

1 Can you see your face? (in groups of four or five)

Some people worry about how they look to others; some do not. Try
Cassius' question (line 51) on unsuspecting friends. Report back on
their responses and how a man like Cassius could exploit them, then
guess at Cassius' thoughts in the long pause at line 54.

2 The friendship between Brutus and Cassius (in pairs)

What do the actors in this 2006 RSC production suggest is the nature
of the friendship between Brutus (left) and Cassius?

Sit facing each other and experiment with speaking lines 79–84 in
different ways. What is Cassius' response to Brutus' remark about
the shouting? How close do you feel their friendship is?

cogitations thoughts	**a common laughter** a laughing-stock,
yoke state of slavery	figure of fun
glass mirror	**stale** devalue
jealous on suspicious of	**the rout** the common rabble
	Flourish fanfare of trumpets

CASSIUS Then, Brutus, I have much mistook your passion,
By means whereof this breast of mine hath buried
Thoughts of great value, worthy cogitations.   50
Tell me, good Brutus, can you see your face?

BRUTUS No, Cassius, for the eye sees not itself
But by reflection, by some other things.

CASSIUS 'Tis just,
And it is very much lamented, Brutus,   55
That you have no such mirrors as will turn
Your hidden worthiness into your eye
That you might see your shadow. I have heard
Where many of the best respect in Rome
(Except immortal Caesar), speaking of Brutus   60
And groaning underneath this age's yoke,
Have wished that noble Brutus had his eyes.

BRUTUS Into what dangers would you lead me, Cassius,
That you would have me seek into myself
For that which is not in me?   65

CASSIUS Therefore, good Brutus, be prepared to hear.
And since you know you cannot see yourself
So well as by reflection, I, your glass,
Will modestly discover to yourself
That of yourself which you yet know not of.   70
And be not jealous on me, gentle Brutus,
Were I a common laughter, or did use
To stale with ordinary oaths my love
To every new protester. If you know
That I do fawn on men and hug them hard   75
And after scandal them, or if you know
That I profess myself in banqueting
To all the rout, then hold me dangerous.

Flourish and shout

BRUTUS What means this shouting? I do fear the people
Choose Caesar for their king.

CASSIUS   Ay, do you fear it?   80
Then must I think you would not have it so.

BRUTUS I would not, Cassius, yet I love him well.
But wherefore do you hold me here so long?
What is it that you would impart to me?

Brutus demands that Cassius come to the point. Cassius proclaims that no man of honour should submit to Caesar. He is a mortal but behaves as if he were a god.

---

1 Brutus' honour (in pairs)

Take turns to read Brutus' lines 85–9, in which he states quite clearly his commitment to 'the general good' of Rome and to the concept of 'honour'. Talk together about Brutus' principles – and why they would make it so hard for him to submit to 'immortal Caesar' (line 60).

2 'And this man / Is now become a god' (in groups of about six)

Cassius' long speech (lines 90–131) is an attempt to reveal the ordinary human frailty of Caesar. The people may treat him like a god but:

- Cassius had to save Caesar from drowning in a swimming contest (lines 100–15)
- Caesar behaved in an unbecoming way (like 'a sick girl') when he contracted a fever in Spain (lines 119–28).

One of you plays the silent Brutus. The others share out the lines of Cassius' speech and experiment with different ways of delivering them to Brutus in order to convey Cassius' contempt for Caesar.

Afterwards, Brutus shares with the group his response to Cassius' words. How far has the Cassius group convinced you that Caesar is 'A man of such a feeble temper' (line 129) that he does not deserve the god-like adoration he receives?

---

outward favour external appearance
as lief rather
chafing with battering against
Accoutred dressed
stemming battling against
Aeneas legendary founder of Rome (see p. 171)
Anchises Aeneas' father

If it be aught toward the general good,   85
Set honour in one eye and death i'th'other
And I will look on both indifferently.
For let the gods so speed me as I love
The name of honour more than I fear death.
CASSIUS I know that virtue to be in you, Brutus,   90
As well as I do know your outward favour.
Well, honour is the subject of my story:
I cannot tell what you and other men
Think of this life, but for my single self
I had as lief not be as live to be   95
In awe of such a thing as I myself.
I was born free as Caesar, so were you;
We both have fed as well, and we can both
Endure the winter's cold as well as he.
For once, upon a raw and gusty day,   100
The troubled Tiber chafing with her shores,
Caesar said to me, 'Dar'st thou, Cassius, now
Leap in with me into this angry flood
And swim to yonder point?' Upon the word,
Accoutred as I was, I plungèd in   105
And bade him follow; so indeed he did.
The torrent roared, and we did buffet it
With lusty sinews, throwing it aside
And stemming it with hearts of controversy.
But ere we could arrive the point proposed,   110
Caesar cried, 'Help me, Cassius, or I sink!'
Ay, as Aeneas, our great ancestor,
Did from the flames of Troy upon his shoulder
The old Anchises bear, so from the waves of Tiber
Did I the tired Caesar. And this man   115
Is now become a god, and Cassius is
A wretched creature and must bend his body
If Caesar carelessly but nod on him.
He had a fever when he was in Spain,
And when the fit was on him I did mark   120
How he did shake. 'Tis true, this god did shake,
His coward lips did from their colour fly,

Brutus thinks the offstage shouts mean honours for Caesar. Cassius mocks Caesar's greatness and tries to spur Brutus to action by reminding him that his qualities rank equally with Caesar's.

1 Greatness (whole class)

A visit by a popular and well-known person, especially royalty, creates an expectant atmosphere. That person rivets everyone's attention. Everybody smiles and laughs.

Re-create this atmosphere in your classroom. One person plays top royalty on a visit, other students form their entourage. Plan the visit together in some detail before you play it.

Afterwards, talk together in small groups about how your 'royal visit' reflects Cassius' views in lines 135–61.

2 Cassius, the public speaker (in groups of four or five)

In lines 135–61 Cassius again stresses that Caesar is merely a man like all other men. The words ('man'/'men') resonate through his speech as he first asks Brutus why Caesar is 'grown so great' and attempts to weigh the power and importance of Brutus' name against Caesar's. Finally, Cassius appeals to Brutus' awareness of his proud ancestors who drove the Tarquin kings from Rome and founded the Republic.

Imagine Cassius delivering his speech at a big political rally. His voice is amplified through four big speakers 100 metres apart. Listeners hear the nearest speaker, and then 'echoes' from the other three. Particular words and phrases linger in the air . . . Place a group member in a corner of the room and, as one speaks lines 135–61, the others echo key ideas and phrases.

3 What about Brutus?

Except for his apprehensive response to the offstage shouts for Caesar, Brutus says nothing else during Cassius' long speech (lines 90–161). Write notes for the actor playing Brutus, indicating clearly how he should use movement and gesture at key points to signal his character's feelings.

---

bear the palm   win the victor's trophy
Colossus   giant statue (see p. 172)
start   conjure up

great flood   biblical flood that engulfed the entire world
brooked   tolerated

And that same eye whose bend doth awe the world
Did lose his lustre. I did hear him groan,
Ay, and that tongue of his that bade the Romans   125
Mark him and write his speeches in their books,
'Alas', it cried, 'give me some drink, Titinius',
As a sick girl. Ye gods, it doth amaze me
A man of such a feeble temper should
So get the start of the majestic world   130
And bear the palm alone.
                    Shout. Flourish
BRUTUS Another general shout!
        I do believe that these applauses are
        For some new honours that are heaped on Caesar.
CASSIUS Why, man, he doth bestride the narrow world   135
        Like a Colossus, and we petty men
        Walk under his huge legs and peep about
        To find ourselves dishonourable graves.
        Men at some time are masters of their fates:
        The fault, dear Brutus, is not in our stars   140
        But in ourselves, that we are underlings.
        Brutus and Caesar: what should be in that 'Caesar'?
        Why should that name be sounded more than yours?
        Write them together, yours is as fair a name;
        Sound them, it doth become the mouth as well;   145
        Weigh them, it is as heavy; conjure with 'em,
        'Brutus' will start a spirit as soon as 'Caesar'.
        Now in the names of all the gods at once,
        Upon what meat doth this our Caesar feed
        That he is grown so great? Age, thou art shamed! 150
        Rome, thou hast lost the breed of noble bloods!
        When went there by an age since the great flood
        But it was famed with more than with one man?
        When could they say, till now, that talked of Rome,
        That her wide walks encompassed but one man?   155
        Now is it Rome indeed and room enough
        When there is in it but one only man.
        O, you and I have heard our fathers say
        There was a Brutus once that would have brooked
        Th'eternal devil to keep his state in Rome   160
        As easily as a king.

Brutus says he will think about what Cassius has said. Caesar returns, looking angry. He confides to Antony that he is suspicious of Cassius.

---

1 Brutus the 'son of Rome'

To a true aristocrat, honour is more important than life, as Brutus has already said at lines 85–9. He reinforces that view at lines 172–5. As a staunch Republican he will resist any tyranny that might result from Caesar's becoming king.

Write a short paragraph summing up what you have seen so far of Brutus' 'honour' and why you think it is so important to him.

2 Caesar's secret police (in pairs)

Imagine that you are Caesar's intelligence agents who have shadowed Brutus and Cassius through lines 25–177 and bugged their conversation, in order to make a report on them to your master. Examine their words with care before you draw your conclusions. Also remember how they looked and acted as they spoke the most important parts of their conversation. Then make your report to Caesar.

3 Two newspaper photographs of Caesar's displeasure (whole class)

One half of your class arranges itself into a 'photograph' taken at a particular moment during lines 183–8. The other half of the class shows lines 194–5. Refer to the start of the scene for a list of the people in Caesar's train.

When your group has prepared your 'photograph', 'freeze' your pose while the other group tries to work out who is who.

---

nothing jealous   not at all doubtful
meet   appropriate
villager   (i.e. not a Roman citizen)
TRAIN   attendants
chidden   scolded

Cicero   great Republican orator (see p. 171)
crossed in conference   opposed in debate
well given   friendly

BRUTUS That you do love me, I am nothing jealous;
      What you would work me to, I have some aim.
      How I have thought of this, and of these times,
      I shall recount hereafter. For this present,   165
      I would not (so with love I might entreat you)
      Be any further moved. What you have said
      I will consider; what you have to say
      I will with patience hear and find a time
      Both meet to hear and answer such high things.   170
      Till then, my noble friend, chew upon this:
      Brutus had rather be a villager
      Than to repute himself a son of Rome
      Under these hard conditions as this time
      Is like to lay upon us.   175
CASSIUS I am glad that my weak words
      Have struck but thus much show of fire from Brutus.

Enter CAESAR *and his* TRAIN

BRUTUS The games are done and Caesar is returning.
CASSIUS As they pass by, pluck Casca by the sleeve
      And he will (after his sour fashion) tell you   180
      What hath proceeded worthy note today.
BRUTUS I will do so. But look you, Cassius,
      The angry spot doth glow on Caesar's brow
      And all the rest look like a chidden train:
      Calpurnia's cheek is pale, and Cicero   185
      Looks with such ferret and such fiery eyes
      As we have seen him in the Capitol,
      Being crossed in conference by some senators.
CASSIUS Casca will tell us what the matter is.
CAESAR Antonio.   190
ANTONY Caesar.
CAESAR Let me have men about me that are fat,
      Sleek-headed men and such as sleep a-nights.
      Yond Cassius has a lean and hungry look,
      He thinks too much: such men are dangerous.   195
ANTONY Fear him not, Caesar, he's not dangerous,
      He is a noble Roman and well given.

Caesar tells Antony that Cassius is restless, brooding and dangerous. He then departs. Casca confides to Brutus and Cassius that Caesar refused a crown three times at the races.

1 Would he were fatter!

a Experiment with different ways of speaking everything Caesar says in lines 192–214. For example, is Caesar utterly confident and self-assured (he insists twice that he does not personally fear Cassius) or is he unsure of himself and secretly fearful of Cassius? Why do you think Shakespeare adds the detail about Caesar's deafness?

b Make a list of each description of Cassius in lines 192–214, for example 'a lean and hungry look', and so on. Use your list to identify a modern actor (on film, television or stage) who you think would play Cassius well.

2 Cassius at home (in groups of four or five)

We later see Brutus and Caesar at home but never Cassius. Plutarch's *History* tells us that he had a wife and a teenage son but gives no further family details.

Write or improvise a modern-day scene in which Cassius and his family entertain Casca at home. Make use of your knowledge of Cassius, but add your own details.

3 The people respond to Caesar (in groups of three)

Quickly read through lines 220–76, in which Casca reports what has happened at the Lupercal games. Concentrate on how the crowd (Casca calls them 'rabblement', line 240) responds to Caesar, especially when Caesar thrice declines the offer of a crown. Write down all the words and phrases that Casca uses to describe the people and what those words suggest about Casca's attitude to the common people.

Talk together about why you think Shakespeare chooses not to show this scene but has Casca report it.

---

sort manner
chanced happened

sad serious and sullen
gentle noble, kind, refined

CAESAR Would he were fatter! But I fear him not.
        Yet if my name were liable to fear
        I do not know the man I should avoid   200
        So soon as that spare Cassius. He reads much,
        He is a great observer, and he looks
        Quite through the deeds of men. He loves no plays,
        As thou dost, Antony, he hears no music;
        Seldom he smiles, and smiles in such a sort   205
        As if he mocked himself and scorned his spirit
        That could be moved to smile at any thing.
        Such men as he be never at heart's ease
        Whiles they behold a greater than themselves,
        And therefore are they very dangerous.   210
        I rather tell thee what is to be feared
        Than what I fear: for always I am Caesar.
        Come on my right hand, for this ear is deaf,
        And tell me truly what thou think'st of him.
                    Sennet. Exeunt Caesar and his train

CASCA You pulled me by the cloak, would you speak with me?   215
BRUTUS Ay, Casca, tell us what hath chanced today
        That Caesar looks so sad.
CASCA Why, you were with him, were you not?
BRUTUS I should not then ask, Casca, what had chanced.
CASCA Why, there was a crown offered him, and being offered him he put   220
    it by with the back of his hand thus, and then the people fell
    a-shouting.
BRUTUS What was the second noise for?
CASCA Why, for that too.
CASSIUS They shouted thrice; what was the last cry for?   225
CASCA Why, for that too.
BRUTUS Was the crown offered him thrice?
CASCA Ay, marry, was't, and he put it by thrice, every time gentler than
    other; and at every putting-by mine honest neighbours shouted.
CASSIUS Who offered him the crown?   230
CASCA Why, Antony.
BRUTUS Tell us the manner of it, gentle Casca.

Casca describes how Caesar had an epileptic fit after Antony offered him the crown. After that, Caesar offered his bared throat for the crowd to cut.

1 Life, death and honour (in groups of three)

Romans believed that to be honourable, you must hold life lightly: 'there are conditions on which life is not worth having', as Aristotle the Greek philosopher said. Cassius and other major characters wilfully endanger or offer to give up their lives on many occasions, as Caesar does here when he 'offered them his throat to cut'.

Always question what characters really want on these occasions, and what is revealed about their personalities. Explore your own feelings about the value of life, death and honour through improvisation. Choose as your starting point a character who faces an agonising moral dilemma.

2 The crown thrice refused (whole class)

Study Casca's account of how Mark Antony offered a crown to Caesar (lines 233–44). Then, with a Caesar and an Antony, act out the incident at a slow pace while two to three reporters take it in turns to speak a running commentary into an imaginary tape recorder. The rest of the class are the crowd in groups of three or four as families and knots of friends who all have names and different occupations. During and after the incident (which, of course, is punctuated by the cheers of the crowd), the reporters may conduct interviews as they move around, asking in particular for views about kingship. Antony's account of his motives will be of special interest.

3 Caesar's epilepsy

Casca reports (lines 246–7) that Caesar had what sounds like an epileptic fit in the market-place. What do you think this detail adds to the portrait of Caesar that Shakespeare is building up in this scene?

---

fain gladly
chopped chapped, roughened
swounded fainted
the falling sickness epileptic fits
Marry indeed

doublet Elizabethan jacket
And I . . . of any occupation If I had been a man of action
infirmity sickness (i.e. his epilepsy)

CASCA I can as well be hanged as tell the manner of it. It was mere foolery, I did not mark it. I saw Mark Antony offer him a crown – yet 'twas not a crown neither, 'twas one of these coronets – and, as I told you, he 235 put it by once; but for all that, to my thinking he would fain have had it. Then he offered it to him again; then he put it by again; but to my thinking he was very loath to lay his fingers off it. And then he offered it the third time; he put it the third time by, and still as he refused it, the rabblement hooted, and clapped their chopped hands, and threw 240 up their sweaty nightcaps, and uttered such a deal of stinking breath because Caesar refused the crown that it had, almost, choked Caesar, for he swounded and fell down at it. And for mine own part I durst not laugh for fear of opening my lips and receiving the bad air.

CASSIUS But soft, I pray you; what, did Caesar swound? 245

CASCA He fell down in the market-place, and foamed at mouth, and was speechless.

BRUTUS 'Tis very like, he hath the falling sickness.

CASSIUS No, Caesar hath it not, but you, and I,
　　　　And honest Casca, we have the falling sickness. 250

CASCA I know not what you mean by that, but I am sure Caesar fell down. If the tag-rag people did not clap him and hiss him according as he pleased and displeased them, as they use to do the players in the theatre, I am no true man.

BRUTUS What said he when he came unto himself? 255

CASCA Marry, before he fell down, when he perceived the common herd was glad he refused the crown, he plucked me ope his doublet and offered them his throat to cut. And I had been a man of any occupation, if I would not have taken him at a word I would I might go to hell among the rogues. And so he fell. When he came to himself 260 again, he said if he had done or said anything amiss, he desired their worships to think it was his infirmity. Three or four wenches where I stood cried, 'Alas, good soul', and forgave him with all their hearts. But there's no heed to be taken of them: if Caesar had stabbed their mothers they would have done no less. 265

BRUTUS And after that he came thus sad away?

CASCA Ay.

CASSIUS Did Cicero say anything?

CASCA Ay, he spoke Greek.

CASSIUS To what effect? 270

Cassius invites Casca to supper. Brutus invites Cassius to his house. Cassius, alone, tells how he will turn Brutus against Caesar.

1 Conspirators as future rulers – the right stuff?
(in pairs or groups of three)

Old-style Republicans educated their sons at home. Intellectuals like Cicero sent their sons to Athens. They believed the Greeks were culturally superior to the proud but uncultivated citizens of Rome. Some argued that gentry (high-status persons) would be corrupted by mixing with inferior people at school and should have home tutors.

a Talk together about whether you believe it is best 'That noble minds keep ever with their likes'. Does mixing with other people corrupt or benefit those born with high status?

b Casca is introduced to Brutus as the sort of man Cassius wants to recruit for the conspiracy, but Brutus seems doubtful about him. Has the shrewd Cassius misjudged how they might get on together? What might Brutus be thinking about Casca and Cassius during the pause at the end of line 291?

c Conduct separate interviews with Brutus and Cassius about Casca as a potential conspirator.

2 Cassius' and Brutus' private thoughts (in pairs)

a Cassius' soliloquy (lines 297–311) reveals his true thoughts about the noble Brutus and the way Brutus' mind can be 'seduced' into conspiring against Caesar. Take it in turns to try different readings of Cassius' speech and settle on one version that you think appropriately conveys Cassius' state of mind and his scheming intentions.

b Imagine that Shakespeare had given Brutus his own soliloquy in which he reflects on the events of this scene. Write it, and then compare your pair's version with those of other pairs in your class.

---

and I tell   if I tell
quick mettle   a lively character
tardy form   appearance of stupidity
honourable metal   noble qualities
bear me hard   dislike me

several hands   different handwritings
tending   referring
glancèd at   mentioned in passing
seat him sure   make sure he is safe and secure

CASCA Nay, and I tell you that, I'll ne'er look you i'th'face again. But those that understood him smiled at one another and shook their heads; but for mine own part it was Greek to me. I could tell you more news too. Murellus and Flavius, for pulling scarves off Caesar's images, are put to silence. Fare you well. There was more foolery yet, 275 if I could remember it.

CASSIUS Will you sup with me tonight, Casca?

CASCA No, I am promised forth.

CASSIUS Will you dine with me tomorrow?

CASCA Ay, if I be alive, and your mind hold, and your dinner worth the 280 eating.

CASSIUS Good, I will expect you.

CASCA Do so. Farewell both. *Exit*

BRUTUS What a blunt fellow is this grown to be!
    He was quick mettle when he went to school. 285

CASSIUS So is he now in execution
    Of any bold or noble enterprise,
    However he puts on this tardy form.
    This rudeness is a sauce to his good wit,
    Which gives men stomach to digest his words 290
    With better appetite.

BRUTUS And so it is. For this time I will leave you.
    Tomorrow if you please to speak with me,
    I will come home to you; or if you will,
    Come home to me and I will wait for you. 295

CASSIUS I will do so. Till then, think of the world. *Exit Brutus*
    Well, Brutus, thou art noble; yet I see
    Thy honourable metal may be wrought
    From that it is disposed. Therefore it is meet
    That noble minds keep ever with their likes; 300
    For who so firm that cannot be seduced?
    Caesar doth bear me hard, but he loves Brutus.
    If I were Brutus now and he were Cassius,
    He should not humour me. I will this night,
    In several hands, in at his windows throw, 305
    As if they came from several citizens,
    Writings, all tending to the great opinion
    That Rome holds of his name, wherein obscurely
    Caesar's ambition shall be glancèd at.
    And after this let Caesar seat him sure, 310
    For we will shake him, or worse days endure. *Exit*

Casca meets Cicero and describes the natural and supernatural wonders he sees in the tempest which rages. Casca thinks they are bad omens.

---

1 All in a change of scene (in groups of five or six)

Shakespeare's scene changes can be very dramatic moments and often highlight major themes of the plays. Here, the crowds and daylight of Scene 2 give way to night, fierce storms and solitary frightened figures.

Cast and act out the last two lines of Act 1 Scene 2 and the first four of Scene 3 up to 'unfirm'. Three of you act, two provide sound effects; director optional. Note that Casca carries his sword (line 19).

Now imagine you were switching channels on television and this changing sequence is all you saw. Make a list of everything you might suppose about the characters, the situation, the circumstances of the action and the play as a whole.

2 The prodigies – a big production number! (in groups of eight or more)

Combine speech, action and sound effects to present Casca's terrible visions in lines 15–32. Speak individually or together. Move around the room if you can to heighten the effect. In groups of three or four, each take a short passage; you can learn it and be free of the script.

3 Prodigies on the wall (whole class in five groups)

Five prodigies are described by Casca (lines 15–32). Imagine they took place in your neighbourhood yesterday. For a wall display, each group should take a single prodigy and:

- report the prodigy, filled out with vivid details, interviews and comments from people you know
- draw or paint it on a large sheet of paper
- as augurers (interpreters of signs) explain what the gods are telling the people in your neighbourhood through the prodigies.

---

sway kingdom, dominion
rived split
saucy insolent, defiant
sensible of feeling
Against beside

glazed upon stared at
prodigies wondrous sights
(interpreted as omens of the future)
conjointly together, in conjunction
portentous hugely important

Act 1 Scene 3
Rome A street Night

Thunder and lightning. Enter [from opposite sides] CASCA and
                    CICERO

CICERO Good even, Casca, brought you Caesar home?
        Why are you breathless, and why stare you so?
CASCA Are not you moved when all the sway of earth
        Shakes like a thing unfirm? O Cicero,
        I have seen tempests when the scolding winds   5
        Have rived the knotty oaks, and I have seen
        Th'ambitious ocean swell, and rage, and foam,
        To be exalted with the threatening clouds;
        But never till tonight, never till now,
        Did I go through a tempest dropping fire.   10
        Either there is a civil strife in heaven,
        Or else the world, too saucy with the gods,
        Incenses them to send destruction.
CICERO Why, saw you anything more wonderful?
CASCA A common slave – you know him well by sight –   15
        Held up his left hand, which did flame and burn
        Like twenty torches joined, and yet his hand,
        Not sensible of fire, remained unscorched.
        Besides – I ha' not since put up my sword –
        Against the Capitol I met a lion   20
        Who glazed upon me and went surly by
        Without annoying me. And there were drawn
        Upon a heap a hundred ghastly women,
        Transformèd with their fear, who swore they saw
        Men, all in fire, walk up and down the streets.   25
        And yesterday the bird of night did sit
        Even at noon-day upon the market-place,
        Hooting and shrieking. When these prodigies
        Do so conjointly meet let not men say,
        'These are their reasons, they are natural',   30
        For I believe they are portentous things
        Unto the climate that they point upon.

Cicero warns Casca that omens can be misinterpreted. Cassius enters, bare-chested. He welcomes the tempest and despises Casca's fear.

1 Cicero and Casca – in or out of the conspiracy? (in pairs)

Cicero and Casca's opening exchange presents a contrast in their respective characters. Cicero is calm, seeing nothing extraordinary in the storm's power, carefully avoiding political discussion. Casca is disturbed, deeply affected by the omens of the storm that he has seen, and anxious that they signify threat to Rome.

- Take parts and read lines 1–40. How will you bring out their different personalities and viewpoints?
- This is Cicero's last appearance in the play; Brutus later sees him as an unsuitable member of the conspiracy and rejects him, while Casca is accepted. Discuss how actors might play these two roles to highlight the contrasting fates of the two men.

2 Entries in night and tempest (in groups of three or four)

Think carefully about how Cassius enters after line 40. How does Casca greet him? Act out different versions of Cassius' arrival on stage and the four lines that follow it. Talk together about which you felt worked best and why.

Finally, choose any character you have met so far in the play. Walk across the room in the manner your character would move through a tempest. The group guesses which character you have chosen.

3 The world through Cassius' eyes (in pairs)

Read over the quickfire dialogue in lines 41–5 carefully, for meaning. Hold an interview with Cassius as to why the night is pleasing 'to honest men' and why those who find 'the earth so full of faults' find the heavens menacing.

---

strange-disposèd disturbed
thus unbracèd with doublet undone
cross forked
tempt provoke

want lack
from quality and kind depart from their true natures

CICERO   Indeed, it is a strange-disposèd time.
　　　　But men may construe things after their fashion
　　　　Clean from the purpose of the things themselves.　　　　35
　　　　Comes Caesar to the Capitol tomorrow?
CASCA   He doth, for he did bid Antonio
　　　　Send word to you he would be there tomorrow.
CICERO   Good night then, Casca. This disturbèd sky
　　　　Is not to walk in.
CASCA　　　　　　　　Farewell, Cicero.　　　　　　　　40

　　　　　　　　　　　　　　　　　　　　Exit Cicero

　　　　　　　Enter CASSIUS

CASSIUS   Who's there?
CASCA　　　　　　　A Roman.
CASSIUS　　　　　　　　　　Casca, by your voice.
CASCA   Your ear is good. Cassius, what night is this!
CASSIUS   A very pleasing night to honest men.
CASCA   Who ever knew the heavens menace so?
CASSIUS   Those that have known the earth so full of faults.　　45
　　　　For my part I have walked about the streets,
　　　　Submitting me unto the perilous night,
　　　　And, thus unbracèd, Casca, as you see,
　　　　Have bared my bosom to the thunderstone;
　　　　And when the cross blue lightning seemed to open　　50
　　　　The breast of heaven, I did present myself
　　　　Even in the aim and very flash of it.
CASCA   But wherefore did you so much tempt the heavens?
　　　　It is the part of men to fear and tremble
　　　　When the most mighty gods by tokens send　　　　55
　　　　Such dreadful heralds to astonish us.
CASSIUS   You are dull, Casca, and those sparks of life
　　　　That should be in a Roman you do want,
　　　　Or else you use not. You look pale, and gaze,
　　　　And put on fear, and cast yourself in wonder　　　　60
　　　　To see the strange impatience of the heavens.
　　　　But if you would consider the true cause
　　　　Why all these fires, why all these gliding ghosts,
　　　　Why birds and beasts from quality and kind,
　　　　Why old men, fools, and children calculate,　　　　65

Cassius hints that the tempest is a warning that should rouse the people of Rome. Casca tells him that outside Italy, Caesar will be king. Death will free me from such oppression, riddles Cassius.

1 The voice of the tempest (in groups of four to six)

When Cassius talks to Casca, it is as if he reports what the tempest has told him.

Examine lines 62–111 carefully and work out the essence of what Cassius is saying. Then write or improvise a scene in which the tempest talks to him about Caesar, Rome and the strength of spirit. You could work it up into a magnificent presentation!

2 The power of Cassius' spirit (in groups of up to seven)

Working in pairs or groups of three, imagine that one of you is a magician with immense powers of control in your hand. Without speech, use your imagined powers to guide and control the movement of your subject(s). Swap roles.

Now, while two or three of you play the 'magician's control' game, the other members of the group divide lines 41–130 between them and speak them so as to synchronise with the movements. Speakers and movers should inspire each other. Add sound effects when you are not speaking.

3 Cassius: the power of manhood (in pairs)

Cassius claims that modern Romans lack the courage and heroic qualities of their ancestors (lines 80–4). He sees Roman men as 'womanish' and rather than have his honour tainted he will readily embrace suicide. Talk together about Cassius' attitude to life and to the concept of manhood.

---

ordinance proper, required behaviour
preformèd faculties inborn qualities
prodigious supernaturally threatening
thews muscles

yoke bondage, slavery
sufferance long suffering
bondman slave

Why all these things change from their ordinance,
Their natures, and preformèd faculties,
To monstrous quality – why, you shall find
That heaven hath infused them with these spirits
To make them instruments of fear, and warning   70
Unto some monstrous state.
Now could I, Casca, name to thee a man
Most like this dreadful night,
That thunders, lightens, opens graves, and roars
As doth the lion in the Capitol –   75
A man no mightier than thyself, or me,
In personal action, yet prodigious grown
And fearful, as these strange eruptions are.

CASCA 'Tis Caesar that you mean, is it not, Cassius?

CASSIUS Let it be who it is, for Romans now   80
Have thews and limbs like to their ancestors'.
But, woe the while, our fathers' minds are dead
And we are governed with our mothers' spirits;
Our yoke and sufferance show us womanish.

CASCA Indeed, they say the senators tomorrow   85
Mean to establish Caesar as a king,
And he shall wear his crown by sea and land,
In every place save here in Italy.

CASSIUS I know where I will wear this dagger then:
Cassius from bondage will deliver Cassius.   90
Therein, ye gods, you make the weak most strong;
Therein, ye gods, you tyrants do defeat.
Nor stony tower, nor walls of beaten brass,
Nor airless dungeon, nor strong links of iron,
Can be retentive to the strength of spirit;   95
But life, being weary of these worldly bars,
Never lacks power to dismiss itself.
If I know this, know all the world besides,
That part of tyranny that I do bear
I can shake off at pleasure.
                            Thunder still
CASCA   So can I,   100
So every bondman in his own hand bears
The power to cancel his captivity.

Stung by Cassius' words, Casca commits himself to Caesar's overthrow. Cassius tells him of other conspirators he has recruited. One of them, Cinna, enters looking for Cassius.

1 I am a true Roman

Read Act 1 Scene 2, lines 150–75, and this scene, particularly lines 103–15. Cassius knows what a Roman should be. Write a poem like this one about a slave, starting and ending each verse with 'I am a true Roman'.

> I am a slave
> I too had dignity once, but found peace at the whip's end
> When I let dignity slip and be trampled by the chain gang.
> I am a slave.

2 Recruiting conspirators (in groups of about five)

The other conspirators wait for Cassius at Pompey's Porch.

Imagine you are the conspirators meeting a year after Caesar's assassination. Talk about how you were recruited and your feelings at the time. How do Cassius' methods compare with those of the others?

---

hinds   deer / menial servants
fleering   sneering
Be factious   form a rebel group
Pompey's Porch   the doorway into
  Pompey's theatre

In favour's like   in appearance
  is like
gait   footsteps
incorporate / To   committed to
  supporting

CASSIUS And why should Caesar be a tyrant then?
    Poor man, I know he would not be a wolf
    But that he sees the Romans are but sheep;   105
    He were no lion, were not Romans hinds.
    Those that with haste will make a mighty fire
    Begin it with weak straws. What trash is Rome,
    What rubbish and what offal, when it serves
    For the base matter to illuminate   110
    So vile a thing as Caesar? But, O grief,
    Where hast thou led me? I perhaps speak this
    Before a willing bondman, then I know
    My answer must be made. But I am armed,
    And dangers are to me indifferent.   115
CASCA You speak to Casca, and to such a man
    That is no fleering tell-tale. Hold, my hand.
    Be factious for redress of all these griefs,
    And I will set this foot of mine as far
    As who goes farthest.
CASSIUS   There's a bargain made. 120
    Now know you, Casca, I have moved already
    Some certain of the noblest-minded Romans
    To undergo with me an enterprise
    Of honourable dangerous consequence.
    And I do know by this they stay for me   125
    In Pompey's Porch. For now, this fearful night,
    There is no stir or walking in the streets,
    And the complexion of the element
    In favour's like the work we have in hand,
    Most bloody, fiery, and most terrible.   130

Enter CINNA

CASCA Stand close a while, for here comes one in haste.
CASSIUS 'Tis Cinna, I do know him by his gait.
    He is a friend. Cinna, where haste you so?
CINNA To find out you. Who's that? Metellus Cimber?
CASSIUS No, it is Casca, one incorporate   135
    To our attempts. Am I not stayed for, Cinna?
CINNA I am glad on't. What a fearful night is this!
    There's two or three of us have seen strange sights.

Cassius orders Cinna to leave letters for Brutus in places where he will find them. Cassius says Brutus will join the conspirators tonight. They leave to join the other conspirators and go to Brutus' house.

---

1 Unspoken thoughts (in groups of three)

Cinna's dramatic and hasty arrival signals the gathering momentum of the conspiracy. Take parts and act out lines 131–42 with breathless speed, but emphasise the pause at the start of line 140. Talk together about what is not said, but what is probably in the men's minds.

2 Conspirators in the night

Try to capture, in a picture or poem, the conspirators' frantic activity in the deserted streets of Rome. Use some or all of these vivid images from the play:

fire
spirit
tempest
blood
dagger

3 Facts are facts and books are books (in groups of six)

Shakespeare invented Scene 3. In Plutarch there is only one paragraph of portents (which appear as lines 15–28) and no tempest. The story is not advanced at all by the scene.

Some people today do not like 'historical facts' to be changed when made into films. Similar people in Shakespeare's day objected to the liberties taken by dramatists. Shakespeare worked fast and often wrote or made changes in consultation with his actors. Imagine that his actors meet with a group of such objectors in a tavern after the first night, and explain why their author inserted this scene.

Divide into two groups (actors and objectors). Prepare for the argument by listing justifications and objections for inventing or changing historical events in plays.

---

praetor chief magistrate (Brutus' official title)
Repair go
hie hasten, hurry

countenance (1) face, (2) support
alchemy the ancient science that sought to turn base metals into gold
conceited imagined, understood

CASSIUS Am I not stayed for? Tell me.

CINNA   Yes, you are.
          O Cassius, if you could   140
          But win the noble Brutus to our party –

CASSIUS Be you content. Good Cinna, take this paper
          And look you lay it in the praetor's chair,
          Where Brutus may but find it; and throw this
          In at his window; set this up with wax   145
          Upon old Brutus' statue. All this done,
          Repair to Pompey's Porch, where you shall find us.
          Is Decius Brutus and Trebonius there?

CINNA All but Metellus Cimber, and he's gone
          To seek you at your house. Well, I will hie,   150
          And so bestow these papers as you bade me.

CASSIUS That done, repair to Pompey's Theatre.

                                                    Exit Cinna

          Come, Casca, you and I will yet, ere day,
          See Brutus at his house. Three parts of him
          Is ours already, and the man entire   155
          Upon the next encounter yields him ours.

CASCA O, he sits high in all the people's hearts,
          And that which would appear offence in us
          His countenance, like richest alchemy,
          Will change to virtue and to worthiness.   160

CASSIUS Him and his worth and our great need of him
          You have right well conceited. Let us go,
          For it is after midnight, and ere day
          We will awake him and be sure of him.

                                                    Exeunt

Looking back at Act 1
Activities for groups or individuals

1 From play to novel

Write the events of Scene 1 as the first chapter of a novel. Describe the setting, atmosphere, characters' inner thoughts, and so on. Your dialogue should also suggest the attitude and manners of Rome.

2 Caesar passes (in large groups)

Cast yourselves as the characters in Act 1, except Caesar. Each person chooses one or two lines to sum up what their character thinks of Caesar. Line up with expectant smiles. As you imagine Caesar passing in slow motion, say your line(s) about him, adding gesture and facial expressions to match your words. The rest of the class identifies who plays whom.

3 Costume design

Make notes or sketches of your costume ideas for the characters, including the 'crowd' in Scene 1. You may choose historically authentic designs or, like many modern productions, give the play a contemporary resonance; see pictures on pages v (bottom), viii (top), x and xi in the colour section, and others.

4 Caesar at the Lupercal

Royalty in Shakespeare's day copied the Roman Triumph. They liked, on special occasions, to parade through the streets in a procession of elaborate floats.

- Design a Lupercal float for Caesar which emphasises his triumph and the protection of Rome from evil.
- Queen Elizabeth I was often greeted at the gate of a stately home or a city with a poem written for the occasion. Write a poem to welcome Caesar to the games.

5 Cassius: a case study

What do you make of Cassius? Brutus' close friend seems to be the instigator of the conspiracy and the character who dominates the first act. He has a deep hatred of Caesar that is never really explained. Write a case study of Cassius based on his language, his behaviour and what others have said about him in Act 1.

6 The Soothsayer

Every producer must decide how to present the Soothsayer.

- Study the photograph below. How effective do you find this presentation?
- Outline your own ideas for the Soothsayer in your production of *Julius Caesar*. Decide first whether your staging will be in modern or traditional dress.

Night. In his orchard, Brutus sends Lucius to light his study. He decides that Caesar must die to prevent him from using his new power wrongly.

---

1 Scene changing (in groups of three or four)

Cast yourselves as Cassius, Brutus and Lucius. Have a director or sound-effects person if you wish. Decide how to change the scene from storm-torn street to orchard (Act 1 Scene 3, line 164, to Act 2 Scene 1, line 9).

2 The divided self (in groups of three)

In the old morality plays of Shakespeare's childhood, good and bad angels used to stand either side of a character, persuading them to act virtuously or maliciously. In lines 10–34 there are similar 'voices' persuading Brutus one way, then another. Work out where each voice speaks, and where Brutus weighs up between them. Then act out the lines, giving each voice a definite 'character'.

3 'It must be by his death'

Describe how this actor has sought to convey Brutus' mental anguish as he considers Caesar's growing power and ambition.

---

taper candle	**base degrees** earlier humble way of life
general common good	
craves demands, requires	**prevent** act in anticipation
disjoins separates	**quarrel** concern (about Caesar)
affections emotions	**Will bear no colour** cannot be justified
lowliness humble behaviour	
round rung	**Fashion it thus** argue it this way

Act 2 Scene 1
Brutus' orchard Night

Enter BRUTUS *in his orchard*

BRUTUS What, Lucius, ho!
I cannot by the progress of the stars
Give guess how near to day. Lucius, I say!
I would it were my fault to sleep so soundly.
When, Lucius, when? Awake, I say! What, Lucius!   5

Enter LUCIUS

LUCIUS Called you, my lord?
BRUTUS Get me a taper in my study, Lucius.
When it is lighted, come and call me here.
LUCIUS I will, my lord.   *Exit*
BRUTUS It must be by his death. And for my part   10
I know no personal cause to spurn at him
But for the general. He would be crowned:
How that might change his nature, there's the question.
It is the bright day that brings forth the adder
And that craves wary walking. Crown him that,   15
And then I grant we put a sting in him
That at his will he may do danger with.
Th'abuse of greatness is when it disjoins
Remorse from power. And to speak truth of Caesar,
I have not known when his affections swayed   20
More than his reason. But 'tis a common proof
That lowliness is young ambition's ladder,
Whereto the climber-upward turns his face;
But when he once attains the upmost round
He then unto the ladder turns his back,   25
Looks in the clouds, scorning the base degrees
By which he did ascend. So Caesar may.
Then lest he may, prevent. And since the quarrel
Will bear no colour for the thing he is,
Fashion it thus: that what he is, augmented,   30
Would run to these and these extremities.

Lucius brings Brutus one of Cassius' letters. It strengthens Brutus' resolve to kill Caesar. Lucius reports that tomorrow is 15 March – the Ides of March.

---

1 Cryptic letters (in pairs)

It is usually hard to get politicians to listen. Giant letters, plastic babies, 100-metre strings of sausages – all these have been delivered to the homes of political leaders to make a point.

This letter gets Brutus' attention because it is puzzling or 'cryptic'. It is one among many ('Such instigations'), all apparently by different writers but all in fact written by Cassius.

Help Cassius write two or three letters to Brutus, all prompting Brutus to action, but in different ways.

2 The Ides of March (in groups of three or four)

It is the eve of the Ides of March. Brutus reads one of Cassius' letters by the light of a meteor. By the end of his second soliloquy (lines 44–58) Brutus has resolved to assassinate Caesar.

- Share out Brutus' lines amongst the group. As you read through them, emphasise any shifts in tone (e.g. the movement between questions and commands). Show clearly how you think Brutus' mood gradually changes as he moves towards his final position.
- Read Brutus' first soliloquy (lines 10–34), followed instantly by his second. Write down in your own words the stages of his argument, culminating in his intention to kill Caesar.
- Talk together about how you would stage the 'Knock within' after line 59. How does Brutus respond? Does he know the identity of the knocker? And discuss what you think is the impact of Brutus' admission that he has not slept since Cassius 'did whet me against Caesar'.

---

as his kind   as is its nature
mischievous   dangerous
flint   (for lighting the taper)
exhalations   meteors
Tarquin   (the last tyrant kings of Rome – see p. 2)

If the redress will follow   if you give me your backing
thou receivest . . . full petition   you will get everything you ask for
whet   incite

And therefore think him as a serpent's egg
(Which, hatched, would as his kind grow mischievous)
And kill him in the shell.

Enter LUCIUS

LUCIUS The taper burneth in your closet, sir.   35
  Searching the window for a flint, I found
  This paper, thus sealed up, and I am sure
  It did not lie there when I went to bed.
     Gives him the letter
BRUTUS Get you to bed again, it is not day.
  Is not tomorrow, boy, the Ides of March?   40
LUCIUS I know not, sir.
BRUTUS Look in the calendar and bring me word.
LUCIUS I will, sir.   *Exit*
BRUTUS The exhalations whizzing in the air
  Give so much light that I may read by them.   45
     Opens the letter and reads
  'Brutus, thou sleep'st. Awake, and see thyself!
  Shall Rome, etc. Speak, strike, redress!'
  'Brutus, thou sleep'st. Awake!'
  Such instigations have been often dropped
  Where I have took them up.   50
  'Shall Rome, etc.' Thus must I piece it out:
  Shall Rome stand under one man's awe? What, Rome?
  My ancestors did from the streets of Rome
  The Tarquin drive when he was called a king.
  'Speak, strike, redress!' Am I entreated   55
  To speak and strike? O Rome, I make thee promise,
  If the redress will follow, thou receivest
  Thy full petition at the hand of Brutus.

Enter LUCIUS

LUCIUS Sir, March is wasted fifteen days.
     Knock within
BRUTUS 'Tis good. Go to the gate, somebody knocks.   60
       [*Exit Lucius*]
  Since Cassius first did whet me against Caesar
  I have not slept.

Brutus describes how it feels to have made up one's mind to do a fearful act. Lucius reports the arrival of the disguised conspirators. Brutus muses that conspiracy must always hide its nature.

1 'The interim' (in pairs)

Brutus describes, in lines 63–9, a state of mind most of us go through when we've made our minds up to do an all-important act but have not physically done it. It could be facing up to someone we fear, or going to meet a life-threatening challenge, or changing our lives in a way that may have unpredictable consequences.

- Talk together about such times and how they make you feel. Improvise one of them, showing particularly what effect your state of mind has on those around you.
- Write a poem about Brutus or yourself, expanding his image of a troubled person as a kingdom in revolt.

2 Darkness versus light (in small groups)

Shakespeare deliberately contrasts the youthful innocence of Lucius (whose name is derived from the Latin *lux* meaning 'light') with the dark, furtive thoughts of Brutus. The conspirators keep to the shadows with faces muffled, but Brutus feels the plotters will best 'mask' their true feelings by hiding their true intentions in 'smiles and affability'.

Imagine that you are directing a film version of the play. Focus on the start of this scene up to the conspirators' entrance (line 85). What colours and lighting would you use? *Film noir* (from the French 'black film') uses light to hint at the psychological state of mind of its characters. At what point would Brutus be in the shadows? When would he be in close-up? Discuss your ideas and then write up your notes.

genius and the mortal instruments spirit and body
mo more
mark of favour distinguishing characteristics
visage face

native semblance true appearance
Erebus the dark regions on the way to Hades (Roman hell)
prevention being forestalled and thwarted

Between the acting of a dreadful thing
And the first motion, all the interim is
Like a phantasma or a hideous dream.   65
The genius and the mortal instruments
Are then in council, and the state of a man,
Like to a little kingdom, suffers then
The nature of an insurrection.

Enter LUCIUS

LUCIUS Sir, 'tis your brother Cassius at the door,   70
    Who doth desire to see you.
BRUTUS   Is he alone?
LUCIUS No, sir, there are mo with him.
BRUTUS   Do you know them?
LUCIUS No, sir, their hats are plucked about their ears
    And half their faces buried in their cloaks,
    That by no means I may discover them   75
    By any mark of favour.
BRUTUS   Let 'em enter.

                                   [*Exit Lucius*]

They are the faction. O conspiracy,
Sham'st thou to show thy dang'rous brow by night,
When evils are most free? O then by day
Where wilt thou find a cavern dark enough   80
To mask thy monstrous visage? Seek none, conspiracy,
Hide it in smiles and affability,
For if thou path, thy native semblance on,
Not Erebus itself were dim enough
To hide thee from prevention.   85

Enter the conspirators, CASSIUS, CASCA, DECIUS, CINNA,
    METELLUS, *and* TREBONIUS

CASSIUS I think we are too bold upon your rest.
    Good morrow, Brutus, do we trouble you?
BRUTUS I have been up this hour, awake all night.
    Know I these men that come along with you?
CASSIUS Yes, every man of them; and no man here   90
    But honours you, and every one doth wish

Brutus is introduced to the conspirators. After some secret words with Cassius, he shakes their hands but he rejects the suggestion that they should all swear an oath to kill Caesar.

1 Will Brutus join us? (in pairs)

Talk together about what might be said in Brutus' and Cassius' secret conversation (after line 100), then improvise it.

2 Question Brutus (whole class)

By the time Brutus is introduced to the conspirators, he has clearly assumed the role of leader of the group. Look at how he over-rules Cassius on two separate occasions (the swearing of an oath and Cicero's suitability as a conspirator).

Read from the start of this scene to the departure of the conspirators (line 228). What do you think of Brutus and the enterprise to which he is now committed? One volunteer takes on the role of Brutus, to be questioned ('hot-seated') by the class. If Brutus finds a question too difficult, he should say 'Time out', and possible answers can then be discussed by everyone.

3 Cassius' oath (in groups of three)

Cassius never gets to swear his resolution (line 113). Discuss what it might have been and write it down (in not more than two lines). Each group shares its version of Cassius' oath with the class. This will give you many ideas about Cassius and the conspiracy.

4 Rhetorical questions: the power of language

As Brutus rejects the need for the conspirators to swear an oath to each other (lines 119–28), he uses three rhetorical questions (i.e. questions not requiring an answer – see p. 186) to clinch his argument. Collect modern real-life examples of this persuasive technique at work (e.g. listen to teachers, politicians, advertisements).

---

fret   cut ornamental patterns into
Weighing   considering
betimes   immediately
by lottery   by chance
prick us   spur us on, incite us

palter   say one thing and mean another
honesty   honour
engaged   pledged, promised
fall   die

You had but that opinion of yourself
Which every noble Roman bears of you.
This is Trebonius.
BRUTUS   He is welcome hither.
CASSIUS This, Decius Brutus.
BRUTUS   He is welcome too.   95
CASSIUS This, Casca; this, Cinna; and this, Metellus Cimber.
BRUTUS They are all welcome.
        What watchful cares do interpose themselves
        Betwixt your eyes and night?
CASSIUS Shall I entreat a word?   100

                         They whisper

DECIUS Here lies the east, doth not the day break here?
CASCA No.
CINNA O, pardon, sir, it doth, and yon grey lines
       That fret the clouds are messengers of day.
CASCA You shall confess that you are both deceived.   105
       Here, as I point my sword, the sun arises,
       Which is a great way growing on the south,
       Weighing the youthful season of the year.
       Some two months hence, up higher toward the north
       He first presents his fire, and the high east   110
       Stands, as the Capitol, directly here.
BRUTUS [*Advancing with Cassius*] Give me your hands all over, one by
        one.
CASSIUS And let us swear our resolution.
BRUTUS No, not an oath! If not the face of men,
        The sufferance of our souls, the time's abuse –   115
        If these be motives weak, break off betimes,
        And every man hence to his idle bed;
        So let high-sighted tyranny range on,
        Till each man drop by lottery. But if these
        (As I am sure they do) bear fire enough   120
        To kindle cowards and to steel with valour
        The melting spirits of women, then, countrymen,
        What need we any spur but our own cause
        To prick us to redress? What other bond
        Than secret Romans that have spoke the word   125
        And will not palter? And what other oath
        Than honesty to honesty engaged
        That this shall be or we will fall for it?

No oaths – a Roman's promise is enough, says Brutus. He rejects suggestions
that Cicero be approached or Antony killed.

1 The power of oratory (in pairs)

Brutus claims in lines 129– a… y contemptible people need
to swear oaths. Worthy pe … g for honourable causes do
not need them. In this wav … ates (condemns) oath-taking
and eulogises (praises) su; … :ause without swearing oaths
of loyalty. But every Eliza¹ …)olboy knew from his rhetoric
lessons that, by the same ᴛech … you could eulogise oath-taking
and denigrate any cause tha' … : bound by oaths of loyalty.

See if you can present ł … vith an argument that portrays
oath-taking as necessary anᴄ … ble for all people and all causes.

2 Public relations (in grou,ₚ ₒf four or five)

Metellus sees (line 145) that the conspirators have a public image
problem, and so does Brutus (lines 162–83). In those lines Brutus
shows the conspirators how to think of their task in a high-minded,
noble and honourable way. However, he does not show how to get
the general public to think of the assassination in the same way.

You are a public relations firm sympathetic to the Republican
cause. You have secretly been asked to prepare a 'package', using
all modern forms of media at your disposal, to give an immediate
explanation and justification of the assassination. Outline a PR
campaign that will convince everybody that Caesar's death is the
best thing for Rome. Provide such detail (posters, slogans, etc.) as
you think necessary.

3 What to do about Antony? (in pairs)

Cassius urges that Antony ('A shrewd contriver') should be killed
along with Caesar. Brutus stands against what he sees as unnecessary
additional slaughter, believing Antony to pose no threat once Caesar
is dead. Brutus again wins the argument.

Take parts as Cassius and Brutus and improvise the argument
they might later have in private.

---

cautelous cautious, crafty
carrions people who are half dead
even steadfast, unwavering
insuppressive mettle irrepressible
  nature

a several bastardy an un-Roman act
no whit not at all
contriver plotter
annoy harm

Swear priests and cowards and men cautelous,
Old feeble carrions, and such suffering souls   130
That welcome wrongs: unto bad causes swear
Such creatures as men doubt. But do not stain
The even virtue of our enterprise,
Nor th'insuppressive mettle of our spirits,
To think that or our cause or our performance   135
Did need an oath, when every drop of blood
That every Roman bears, and nobly bears,
Is guilty of a several bastardy
If he do break the smallest particle
Of any promise that hath passed from him.   140

CASSIUS But what of Cicero? Shall we sound him?
I think he will stand very strong with us.

CASCA Let us not leave him out.

CINNA   No, by no means.

METELLUS O, let us have him, for his silver hairs
Will purchase us a good opinion   145
And buy men's voices to commend our deeds.
It shall be said his judgement ruled our hands;
Our youths and wildness shall no whit appear,
But all be buried in his gravity.

BRUTUS O, name him not, let us not break with him,   150
For he will never follow anything
That other men begin.

CASSIUS   Then leave him out.

CASCA Indeed he is not fit.

DECIUS Shall no man else be touched but only Caesar?

CASSIUS Decius, well urged. I think it is not meet   155
Mark Antony, so well beloved of Caesar,
Should outlive Caesar. We shall find of him
A shrewd contriver. And, you know, his means,
If he improve them, may well stretch so far
As to annoy us all, which to prevent,   160
Let Antony and Caesar fall together.

BRUTUS Our course will seem too bloody, Caius Cassius,
To cut the head off and then hack the limbs –
Like wrath in death and envy afterwards –
For Antony is but a limb of Caesar.   165

Brutus says Caesar must be killed, not with spite, but with regret. Again, he overrules Cassius' fears about Antony. Cassius worries that superstition may keep Caesar at home.

---

1 The sacrifice of Caesar (in groups of three or four)

'Let's be sacrificers, but not butchers', says Brutus.

Try several group readings of Brutus' lines 166–80, taking a sentence each and then changing speaker. As you read, emphasise Brutus' vacillating (wavering) thoughts and moods. Is he calm, passionate, imploring, defiant or . . . ?

2 Why should Antony die? (in pairs)

Brutus interrupts Cassius at line 185 and at line 192 the striking clock ends their discussion about whether Antony should also be killed.

- Talk together about the dramatic impact of the clock striking: it is 3 a.m. on the morning of the Ides of March . . .
- Discuss having the clock strike later in order to let Cassius voice his shrewdest suspicions about Antony and his friendship with Caesar. He could change the course of history!

3 Conspirators caught in conspiracy (in pairs or groups of three)

Imagine that Caesar's secret agents, with or without Caesar's knowledge, have bugged Brutus' house. Now with cast-iron proof of conspiracy, they arrest the conspirators and bring them before Caesar for trial.

Construct a case for the conspirators' defence.

---

come by   get possession of
envious   malicious
purgers   healers
engrafted   deeply rooted
much he should   too much for him
  to do

fear   cause for fear
ceremonies   omens
augurers   priests who 'foresaw' the
  future (see p. 171)

Let's be sacrificers, but not butchers, Caius.
We all stand up against the spirit of Caesar,
And in the spirit of men there is no blood.
O, that we then could come by Caesar's spirit
And not dismember Caesar! But, alas,   170
Caesar must bleed for it. And, gentle friends,
Let's kill him boldly, but not wrathfully;
Let's carve him as a dish fit for the gods,
Not hew him as a carcass fit for hounds.
And let our hearts, as subtle masters do,   175
Stir up their servants to an act of rage
And after seem to chide 'em. This shall make
Our purpose necessary, and not envious;
Which so appearing to the common eyes,
We shall be called purgers, not murderers.   180
And for Mark Antony, think not of him,
For he can do no more than Caesar's arm
When Caesar's head is off.
CASSIUS   Yet I fear him,
For in the engrafted love he bears to Caesar –
BRUTUS Alas, good Cassius, do not think of him.   185
If he love Caesar, all that he can do
Is to himself – take thought and die for Caesar;
And that were much he should, for he is given
To sports, to wildness, and much company.
TREBONIUS There is no fear in him, let him not die,   190
For he will live and laugh at this hereafter.
                    Clock strikes
BRUTUS Peace, count the clock.
CASSIUS   The clock hath stricken three.
TREBONIUS 'Tis time to part.
CASSIUS   But it is doubtful yet
Whether Caesar will come forth today or no,
For he is superstitious grown of late,   195
Quite from the main opinion he held once
Of fantasy, of dreams, and ceremonies.
It may be these apparent prodigies,
The unaccustomed terror of this night,
And the persuasion of his augurers   200
May hold him from the Capitol today.

Decius promises to bring Caesar to the Capitol. The conspirators agree to meet at 8 a.m. at Caesar's house. They leave Brutus alone. Portia enters and Brutus questions why she has risen from her bed.

---

1 To catch a toad with a wellington boot (in pairs)

Geffrey Whitney's *A Choice of Emblems* (1586) describes how to catch an elephant. It was believed that elephants had no knee joints and slept leaning on trees. If you weakened the tree beforehand, it would collapse and the elephant would be unable to get up. Explain to each other exactly how you could catch animals using the methods outlined in lines 204–6. Help Decius devise even more absurd superstitions. Write down the best.

2 Brutus, in with us at last! (in groups of three)

The last eight lines of Act 1 Scene 3 showed how much Cassius and Casca wanted Brutus to join the conspiracy. Brutus has now joined.

Hold a conversation between three other conspirators, keyed up about tomorrow, as they walk away from the meeting. They assess how the meeting went and whether Brutus' membership has already changed things, for better or worse.

3 Lucius the silent witness

Lucius has been offstage since line 76 of this scene. Since then the seven conspirators have gathered and made their plans. Imagine that Lucius has overheard most or all of their dialogue. Write his monologue as he takes stock of their meeting. End his account at line 228 as the conspirators leave.

---

o'ersway him   persuade him otherwise
toils   nets
give his humour the true bent   make him think what we want him to think
bear Caesar hard   hate Caesar

rated   criticised
by him   to his house
put on   reveal, betray
formal constancy   dignified behaviour
figures   imaginings

52

DECIUS Never fear that. If he be so resolved
         I can o'ersway him, for he loves to hear
         That unicorns may be betrayed with trees,
         And bears with glasses, elephants with holes,   205
         Lions with toils, and men with flatterers.
         But when I tell him he hates flatterers
         He says he does, being then most flatterèd.
         Let me work:
         For I can give his humour the true bent,   210
         And I will bring him to the Capitol.
CASSIUS Nay, we will all of us be there to fetch him.
BRUTUS By the eighth hour, is that the uttermost?
CINNA Be that the uttermost, and fail not then.
METELLUS Caius Ligarius doth bear Caesar hard,   215
         Who rated him for speaking well of Pompey.
         I wonder none of you have thought of him.
BRUTUS Now, good Metellus, go along by him.
         He loves me well, and I have given him reasons.
         Send him but hither and I'll fashion him.   220
CASSIUS The morning comes upon's. We'll leave you, Brutus,
         And, friends, disperse yourselves, but all remember
         What you have said and show yourselves true Romans.
BRUTUS Good gentlemen, look fresh and merrily:
         Let not our looks put on our purposes,   225
         But bear it as our Roman actors do,
         With untired spirits and formal constancy.
         And so good morrow to you every one.
                              Exeunt [*all but*] *Brutus*
         Boy! Lucius! Fast asleep? It is no matter,
         Enjoy the honey-heavy dew of slumber.   230
         Thou hast no figures nor no fantasies
         Which busy care draws in the brains of men,
         Therefore thou sleep'st so sound.

                       Enter PORTIA

PORTIA   Brutus, my lord.
BRUTUS Portia! What mean you? Wherefore rise you now?
         It is not for your health thus to commit   235
         Your weak condition to the raw cold morning.

Portia tells Brutus how difficult he has been in recent days. He tells her he's sick. She asks why he is out of bed, insisting on the truth.

1 An uncurtained window (in groups of three or four)

As one or two of you read lines 238–51, where Portia describes what happened the previous night ('yesternight'), you pause briefly after each action to allow the other two in the group to act out the scene without sound, as you might see it through an uncurtained window.

2 What's on Brutus' mind? (in groups of four or five)

Brutus says very little to Portia. His mind is probably on the assassination. Gather speeches by Brutus and others about the assassination (Act 1 Scene 2, lines 92–161; Act 2 Scene 1, lines 10–34 and 154–91). Then, while two of you read this part of the scene as Brutus and Portia, the rest of you urgently speak the gathered speeches into Brutus' ear, as if they were Brutus' turbulent thoughts. Brutus' thoughts should vie with Portia's words as determinedly as possible, without physical action or raised voices, to get Brutus' undivided attention.

Afterwards, Brutus can tell you what got through and what it felt like to have so much on his mind.

3 'Upon my knees' (in pairs)

Improvise a situation in which somebody you look up to and respect kneels to ask something of you. That somebody could be a parent, a teacher or someone you admire on television. It is an important matter, not a joke. Discuss how this makes both of you feel.

Now read aloud Portia's plea from line 261 to Brutus' reply (line 278) and work out what is happening between them here.

---

an effect of humour a sign of a passing mood	**humours** unhealthy moisture
come by it get it	**rheumy** moist and catarrhal
physical medically advisable	**sick offence** harmful sickness
unbracèd with clothes undone	**charm** beg, entreat
	incorporate unite, join

PORTIA   Nor for yours neither. Y'have ungently, Brutus,
            Stole from my bed; and yesternight at supper
            You suddenly arose and walked about,
            Musing and sighing, with your arms across,   240
            And when I askèd you what the matter was,
            You stared upon me with ungentle looks.
            I urged you further, then you scratched your head
            And too impatiently stamped with your foot.
            Yet I insisted, yet you answered not,   245
            But with an angry wafture of your hand
            Gave sign for me to leave you. So I did,
            Fearing to strengthen that impatience
            Which seemed too much enkindled, and withal
            Hoping it was but an effect of humour   250
            Which sometime hath his hour with every man.
            It will not let you eat nor talk nor sleep;
            And could it work so much upon your shape
            As it hath much prevailed on your condition,
            I should not know you, Brutus. Dear my lord,   255
            Make me acquainted with your cause of grief.
BRUTUS   I am not well in health, and that is all.
PORTIA   Brutus is wise, and were he not in health
            He would embrace the means to come by it.
BRUTUS   Why, so I do. Good Portia, go to bed.   260
PORTIA   Is Brutus sick? And is it physical
            To walk unbracèd and suck up the humours
            Of the dank morning? What, is Brutus sick?
            And will he steal out of his wholesome bed
            To dare the vile contagion of the night   265
            And tempt the rheumy and unpurgèd air
            To add unto his sickness? No, my Brutus,
            You have some sick offence within your mind,
            Which by the right and virtue of my place
            I ought to know of. And upon my knees   270
            I charm you, by my once commended beauty,
            By all your vows of love, and that great vow
            Which did incorporate and make us one,
            That you unfold to me, your self, your half,

Portia claims that Brutus excludes her. She reveals a self-inflicted wound showing her courage, secrecy and love. Brutus is moved.

1 Portia's wound (in groups of four or five)

You are all Portia, just before she inflicts the thigh wound.

Sit in a circle, each holding an imaginary knife. In turn, speak the thoughts leading to your 'voluntary wound'. When you feel ready, bring the knife down violently on your thigh. Those who do not feel ready continue speaking until they do. When everyone has brought their knife down, talk together about Portia's reasons for injuring herself.

2 Brutus tells all (in pairs)

Later (Act 2 Scene 4, line 9), it seems that Brutus did tell Portia the reasons for his behaviour. Improvise the scene in which he explains all. Portia would probably not let anything go unquestioned. She may have comments and insights about those involved, both conspirators and Caesarites.

3 Brutus and Portia's relationship

What does this picture suggest about the way in which Brutus and Portia relate to each other?

heavy so depressed	**counsels** secrets
excepted acceptable	**constancy** trustworthiness
in sort or limitation only within specific limits	**engagements** dealings
	construe explain, tell (see p. 12)
in the suburbs on the edges	**All the charactery of my sad brows**
harlot mistress, prostitute	all that is written in my sad face
Cato a famous diehard Republican	

Why you are heavy and what men tonight 275
Have had resort to you, for here have been
Some six or seven who did hide their faces
Even from darkness.
BRUTUS   Kneel not, gentle Portia.
PORTIA I should not need if you were gentle Brutus.
Within the bond of marriage, tell me, Brutus, 280
Is it excepted I should know no secrets
That appertain to you? Am I your self
But, as it were, in sort or limitation,
To keep with you at meals, comfort your bed,
And talk to you sometimes? Dwell I but in the suburbs 285
Of your good pleasure? If it be no more
Portia is Brutus' harlot, not his wife.
BRUTUS You are my true and honourable wife,
As dear to me as are the ruddy drops
That visit my sad heart. 290
PORTIA If this were true, then should I know this secret.
I grant I am a woman, but withal
A woman that Lord Brutus took to wife.
I grant I am a woman, but withal
A woman well reputed, Cato's daughter. 295
Think you I am no stronger than my sex,
Being so fathered and so husbanded?
Tell me your counsels, I will not disclose 'em.
I have made strong proof of my constancy,
Giving myself a voluntary wound 300
Here, in the thigh. Can I bear that with patience
And not my husband's secrets?
BRUTUS   O ye gods,
Render me worthy of this noble wife!
                    Knock
Hark, hark, one knocks. Portia, go in a while,
And by and by thy bosom shall partake 305
The secrets of my heart.
All my engagements I will construe to thee,
All the charactery of my sad brows.
Leave me with haste.
                              Exit Portia
             Lucius, who's that knocks?

The sick Ligarius enters. Brutus asks for his help. Ligarius seems to find new strength in being part of the secret enterprise and swears blind obedience to Brutus.

1 Ligarius – more sickness (in pairs)

Sickness is an important dramatic element in the play. There are three separate instances in this scene:

- Brutus' declining psychological health (sleepless nights, troubled mind), which is contrasted with Lucius' restful innocence
- Portia's self-inflicted wound on her thigh
- Ligarius' bodily sickness which is covered by a bandage ('kerchief').

At line 327 Brutus describes the planned assassination of Caesar as 'A piece of work that will make sick men whole.' Talk together about the effects created by the theme of sickness in this scene and then write a short paragraph presenting your ideas. Add further notes on this as you read on through the play.

2 Brutus cures Ligarius (in pairs)

Ligarius' sickness miraculously disappears once he pledges himself to Brutus' cause. Take it in turns to be Ligarius and try different versions of lines 320–6 during which his transformation takes place. Can you present both his physical recovery and his strength of feeling for Brutus, the 'Soul of Rome'?

3 Brutus' night (in groups of three or four)

The scene begins with Brutus wrestling agonisingly with his conscience – and ends with a resolute Brutus, leader of the conspirators. A dramatic and symbolic roll of thunder seems to point inevitably to Caesar's death.

Imagine you are Brutus passing a restless few hours before the dawning of the fateful day. What goes through your mind? Do you look back, or forward? What details will you share with your anguished wife Portia?

Write your thoughts as a 'stream of consciousness' narrative. Let them tumble onto the page.

Vouchsafe good morrow accept my greetings
wear a kerchief be ill
honourable loins a noble family
mortifièd deadened
whole healthy

Enter LUCIUS *and* LIGARIUS

LUCIUS Here is a sick man that would speak with you.   310
BRUTUS Caius Ligarius, that Metellus spake of.
      Boy, stand aside.

                                             [Exit Lucius]

                 Caius Ligarius, how?
LIGARIUS Vouchsafe good morrow from a feeble tongue.
BRUTUS O, what a time have you chose out, brave Caius,
      To wear a kerchief! Would you were not sick!   315
LIGARIUS I am not sick if Brutus have in hand
      Any exploit worthy the name of honour.
BRUTUS Such an exploit have I in hand, Ligarius,
      Had you a healthful ear to hear of it.
LIGARIUS By all the gods that Romans bow before,   320
      I here discard my sickness!
            [He pulls off his kerchief]
                     Soul of Rome,
      Brave son, derived from honourable loins,
      Thou, like an exorcist, hast conjured up
      My mortifièd spirit. Now bid me run
      And I will strive with things impossible,   325
      Yea, get the better of them. What's to do?
BRUTUS A piece of work that will make sick men whole.
LIGARIUS But are not some whole that we must make sick?
BRUTUS That must we also. What it is, my Caius,
      I shall unfold to thee as we are going   330
      To whom it must be done.
LIGARIUS   Set on your foot,
      And with a heart new fired I follow you
      To do I know not what; but it sufficeth
      That Brutus leads me on.
                   Thunder
BRUTUS   Follow me then.

                                     Exeunt

Caesar tells how his wife Calpurnia has spoken of his murder in her sleep. She orders him to stay at home, telling of frightening portents of ill omen. Caesar is unmoved, declaring he will go out.

1 At home with Brutus and Caesar (in groups of three)

Remind yourselves briefly of Act 2 Scene 1, lines 233–309 (Brutus and Portia together) and read through Act 2 Scene 2, lines 1–82 (Caesar and Calpurnia together). Act the two scenes out to another group, if you wish. You could use a director.

Discuss everything you notice that is different about the domestic lives of Brutus and Caesar. Then head up two columns, one with 'Portia' and the other with 'Calpurnia'. Fill in each column with your thoughts about the two women – in what ways are they similar and in what ways different?

2 Always I am Caesar (in groups of four)

Caesar often refers to himself not as 'I' or 'me', but as 'Caesar', even when in conversation with his wife.

Try holding a conversation with your friends in which you always refer to yourself by your surname. Topics can range from what you had for breakfast to your grandest personal ambitions.

Afterwards, talk together about the effect this had on your conversation. Then discuss why Caesar does it.

3 The watch's log

Write the formal report of Caesar's guards (the 'watch') after witnessing the strange and supernatural events described in lines 17–24. What do they make of these ominous visions?

---

nightgown dressing gown	**stood on ceremonies** attached importance to omens
priests (i.e. augurers – see pp. 50, 171)	**watch** night-watchmen
present immediate	**whelpèd** given birth
success the outcome (whether good or bad)	**beyond all use** completely abnormal

Act 2 Scene 2
Caesar's house Early morning

Thunder and lightning. Enter JULIUS CAESAR *in his nightgown*

CAESAR Nor heaven nor earth have been at peace tonight.
Thrice hath Calpurnia in her sleep cried out,
'Help ho, they murder Caesar!' Who's within?

Enter a SERVANT

SERVANT My lord?
CAESAR Go bid the priests do present sacrifice   5
And bring me their opinions of success.
SERVANT I will, my lord.   *Exit*

Enter CALPURNIA

CALPURNIA What mean you, Caesar, think you to walk forth?
You shall not stir out of your house today.
CAESAR Caesar shall forth. The things that threatened me   10
Ne'er looked but on my back; when they shall see
The face of Caesar they are vanishèd.
CALPURNIA Caesar, I never stood on ceremonies,
Yet now they fright me. There is one within,
Besides the things that we have heard and seen,   15
Recounts most horrid sights seen by the watch.
A lioness hath whelpèd in the streets,
And graves have yawned and yielded up their dead;
Fierce fiery warriors fight upon the clouds
In ranks and squadrons and right form of war,   20
Which drizzled blood upon the Capitol;
The noise of battle hurtled in the air,
Horses did neigh and dying men did groan,
And ghosts did shriek and squeal about the streets.
O Caesar, these things are beyond all use,   25
And I do fear them.
CAESAR   What can be avoided
Whose end is purposed by the mighty gods?
Yet Caesar shall go forth, for these predictions
Are to the world in general as to Caesar.

Although Caesar claims to have no fear of death and at first defies Calpurnia and the augurers, in the end their concerns prevail. He orders Decius to tell the Senate that Caesar will not come today.

---

1 Calpurnia's fears for Caesar (in pairs or threes)

It is the morning of the Ides of March. Calpurnia has dreamt all night of her husband's murder. She struggles to persuade Caesar to stay at home.

- Take parts as Caesar, Calpurnia and their servant and read lines 1–56. Emphasise the mental tussling that husband and wife go through. Where does Caesar seem to change his mind and why?
- 'Hot seat' Caesar. Study closely what he says in lines 1–56, then ask him a range of questions designed to expose the man behind the public face and the true reasons for his decision to stay at home.

How does Caesar respond to Calpurnia's pleas in this 2001 RSC production?

---

blaze forth announce
a beast without a heart like a cowardly animal

Your wisdom . . . confidence your self-confidence makes you behave rashly
for thy humour to keep you happy

CALPURNIA When beggars die there are no comets seen, 30
        The heavens themselves blaze forth the death of princes.

CAESAR Cowards die many times before their deaths,
        The valiant never taste of death but once.
        Of all the wonders that I yet have heard
        It seems to me most strange that men should fear, 35
        Seeing that death, a necessary end,
        Will come when it will come.

Enter a SERVANT

                             What say the augurers?

SERVANT They would not have you to stir forth today.
        Plucking the entrails of an offering forth,
        They could not find a heart within the beast. 40

CAESAR The gods do this in shame of cowardice.
        Caesar should be a beast without a heart
        If he should stay at home today for fear.
        No, Caesar shall not. Danger knows full well
        That Caesar is more dangerous than he: 45
        We are two lions littered in one day,
        And I the elder and more terrible.
        And Caesar shall go forth.

CALPURNIA   Alas, my lord,
        Your wisdom is consumed in confidence.
        Do not go forth today. Call it my fear 50
        That keeps you in the house, and not your own.
        We'll send Mark Antony to the Senate House
        And he shall say you are not well today.
        Let me, upon my knee, prevail in this.

CAESAR Mark Antony shall say I am not well, 55
        And for thy humour I will stay at home.

Enter DECIUS

        Here's Decius Brutus, he shall tell them so.

DECIUS Caesar, all hail! Good morrow, worthy Caesar,
        I come to fetch you to the Senate House.

CAESAR And you are come in very happy time 60
        To bear my greeting to the senators
        And tell them that I will not come today.
        Cannot is false, and that I dare not, falser:
        I will not come today. Tell them so, Decius.

Calpurnia suggests that Decius should say Caesar is sick. Caesar scorns the lie and describes Calpurnia's dream. Decius interprets it favourably and says the Senate intend to crown Caesar.

1 'I will not come' (in pairs)

Caesar gives Decius this message for the Senate, explaining why he will not attend the Capitol that day: 'The cause is in my will. I will not come: / That is enough to satisfy the Senate' (lines 71–2).

Read these lines several times to each other, then decide what they show about Caesar's character.

2 The dream interpreted in two ways (two groups of six)

Both Republican conspirators and Caesarites could make use of Calpurnia's prophetic dream to justify or condemn Caesar's assassination after the event.

One group focuses on Calpurnia's interpretation of the dream (lines 76–82). The other concentrates on Decius' explanation (lines 83–90). Each group produces a 'still image' (tableau) of their version. Compare the effects.

3 'Tinctures, stains, relics, and cognisance'

Two ideas are brought together in line 89. Because Caesar is a martyr, relics dipped in his blood are holy. As a prince he dispenses colours or 'tinctures' that can be put on a coat of arms – recognition or 'cognisance' by a royal personage. Both ideas flatter Caesar and both are repugnant to a true Republican.

In medieval England, the Catholic Church put relics of saints in beautiful gold and jewelled boxes called reliquaries. Design a reliquary or a coat of arms which expresses your loyalty to Caesar after his death.

---

greybeards old men
stays me keeps me
lusty healthy, strong
all amiss incorrectly

tinctures, stains, relics, and cognisance (see Activity 3 above)
mock / Apt to be rendered sarcastic remark likely to be made

CALPURNIA Say he is sick.

CAESAR   Shall Caesar send a lie?   65
          Have I in conquest stretched mine arm so far
          To be afeard to tell greybeards the truth?
          Decius, go tell them Caesar will not come.

DECIUS Most mighty Caesar, let me know some cause,
          Lest I be laughed at when I tell them so.   70

CAESAR The cause is in my will. I will not come:
          That is enough to satisfy the Senate.
          But for your private satisfaction,
          Because I love you, I will let you know:
          Calpurnia here, my wife, stays me at home.   75
          She dreamt tonight she saw my statue,
          Which like a fountain with an hundred spouts
          Did run pure blood, and many lusty Romans
          Came smiling and did bathe their hands in it.
          And these does she apply for warnings and portents   80
          And evils imminent, and on her knee
          Hath begged that I will stay at home today.

DECIUS This dream is all amiss interpreted,
          It was a vision fair and fortunate.
          Your statue spouting blood in many pipes,   85
          In which so many smiling Romans bathed,
          Signifies that from you great Rome shall suck
          Reviving blood and that great men shall press
          For tinctures, stains, relics, and cognisance.
          This by Calpurnia's dream is signified.   90

CAESAR And this way have you well expounded it.

DECIUS I have, when you have heard what I can say.
          And know it now: the Senate have concluded
          To give this day a crown to mighty Caesar.
          If you shall send them word you will not come,   95
          Their minds may change. Besides, it were a mock
          Apt to be rendered for someone to say,
          'Break up the Senate till another time,
          When Caesar's wife shall meet with better dreams.'

Caesar finally resolves to go to the Senate. First the conspirators, then Antony arrive. Caesar offers wine while he prepares himself. The conspirators secretly confide their true intentions.

---

1 Decius the persuader (in groups of three)

Decius needs to persuade Caesar to go to the Capitol. Between lines 92 and 104 he marshals three arguments that suggest Caesar should attend. Read his lines to each other several times and identify the three elements of Decius' strategy. Then rank order them: which is the most important in changing Caesar's mind? Compare your thinking with that of other groups.

2 Married to the great (in groups of three)

The careers of major politicians can be made or broken by their spouses.

a Portia and Calpurnia are very different kinds of wife. Imagine they meet at a cocktail party given by Caesar. They talk about their role as the wives of eminent Romans. Bring Cassius' wife in too. Her character will be entirely your own creation.

b When Caesar changes his mind, he claims he is 'ashamed' to have given in to Calpurnia's 'foolish' fears. Does he speak the word in jest, or in earnest? Give your reasons.

3 Murmurs of conspiracy (in groups of four)

At the end of the scene we hear the secret thoughts of the conspirators.

On the way to the Capitol, you and another conspirator lag behind with Decius. You talk, among other things, about how Caesar was persuaded to come to the Senate.

As you talk, Cassius catches up. You ask why he was absent.

---

my . . . To your proceeding   my concern for your future career
reason . . . is liable   my love for you is greater than my judgement
robe   Roman toga
ague   fever

prepare within   (presumably prepare the wine; see line 126)
every like . . . same   being 'like friends' is not the same as being true friends
earns   grieves

If Caesar hide himself, shall they not whisper,   100
'Lo, Caesar is afraid'?
Pardon me, Caesar, for my dear dear love
To your proceeding bids me tell you this,
And reason to my love is liable.
CAESAR How foolish do your fears seem now, Calpurnia!   105
I am ashamèd I did yield to them.
Give me my robe, for I will go.

Enter BRUTUS, *Ligarius, Metellus, Casca,* TREBONIUS, *Cinna, and*
PUBLIUS

And look where Publius is come to fetch me.
PUBLIUS Good morrow, Caesar.
CAESAR   Welcome, Publius.
What, Brutus, are you stirred so early too?   110
Good morrow, Casca. Caius Ligarius,
Caesar was ne'er so much your enemy
As that same ague which hath made you lean.
What is't o'clock?
BRUTUS   Caesar, 'tis strucken eight.
CAESAR I thank you for your pains and courtesy.   115

Enter ANTONY

See, Antony, that revels long a-nights,
Is notwithstanding up. Good morrow, Antony.
ANTONY So to most noble Caesar.
CAESAR [*To Calpurnia*]   Bid them prepare within,
                                    [*Exit Calpurnia*]
I am to blame to be thus waited for.
Now, Cinna, now, Metellus. What, Trebonius,   120
I have an hour's talk in store for you.
Remember that you call on me today;
Be near me that I may remember you.
TREBONIUS Caesar, I will. [*Aside*] And so near will I be
That your best friends shall wish I had been further.   125
CAESAR Good friends, go in and taste some wine with me,
And we, like friends, will straightway go together.
BRUTUS [*Aside*] That every like is not the same, O Caesar,
The heart of Brutus earns to think upon.
                                          Exeunt

Artemidorus reads out the warning he intends to give Caesar. Sending Lucius to the Capitol, Portia confides how she can hardly hide her worries.

1 Artemidorus gives evidence

Imagine you are Artemidorus. Take each or some of the conspirators named in your paper and put together evidence that supports your suspicions about them. You can make up details, but keep close to the spirit of the play. Perhaps you have an informer among the conspirators and have compiled a dossier on each conspirator. Remember that you have signed the paper and your evidence may come up in court.

2 Arguing with the director (in groups A and B of two or three each)

Many directors cut a Shakespeare script to shorten the playing time. Group A are directors who want to cut Act 2 Scenes 3 and 4. Group B are actors in those scenes who protest. Both groups must make their case clearly.

Perhaps other scenes so far in the play should go! If so, which ones?

3 Portia's agitation

Portia, like her husband Brutus in an earlier scene, has troubled thoughts jostling in her mind. Her confidential 'aside' (lines 6–9) suggests that she is desperate to speak of something and finds it incredibly hard to restrain herself.

What do you think is on her mind? It seems to involve sending Lucius on an errand to the Capitol. Read quickly through to the end of the scene for possible clues and then make notes on your ideas. The whole class pools its responses.

---

bent   directed
security . . . conspiracy
  overconfidence leaves you open to
  plots against you
Thy lover   your loyal friend
suitor   petitioner

virtue . . . emulation   virtuous men are
  never beyond the reach of envious
  rivals
contrive   conspire, plot
constancy   self-control
keep counsel   keep a secret

Act 2 Scene 3
Rome A street

Enter ARTEMIDORUS [reading a paper]

ARTEMIDORUS 'Caesar, beware of Brutus, take heed of Cassius, come
not near Casca, have an eye to Cinna, trust not Trebonius, mark well
Metellus Cimber, Decius Brutus loves thee not, thou hast wronged
Caius Ligarius. There is but one mind in all these men, and it is bent
against Caesar. If thou beest not immortal look about you: security
gives way to conspiracy. The mighty gods defend thee!   5
                                                        Thy lover,
                                                        Artemidorus.'

        Here will I stand till Caesar pass along,
        And as a suitor will I give him this.
        My heart laments that virtue cannot live   10
        Out of the teeth of emulation.
        If thou read this, O Caesar, thou mayst live;
        If not, the fates with traitors do contrive.   *Exit*

Act 2 Scene 4
Rome A street

Enter PORTIA and LUCIUS

PORTIA I prithee, boy, run to the Senate House.
        Stay not to answer me but get thee gone.
        Why dost thou stay?
LUCIUS   To know my errand, madam.
PORTIA I would have had thee there and here again
        Ere I can tell thee what thou shouldst do there.   5
        [*Aside*] O constancy, be strong upon my side,
        Set a huge mountain 'tween my heart and tongue!
        I have a man's mind, but a woman's might.
        How hard it is for women to keep counsel! –
        Art thou here yet?
LUCIUS   Madam, what should I do?   10
        Run to the Capitol, and nothing else?
        And so return to you, and nothing else?

Portia sends Lucius to report back to her what Brutus says and does. The Soothsayer foresees harm to Caesar, but crowds make his warning difficult to deliver.

---

1 Listening to the wind (in pairs or groups of three)

Sometimes, when listening for an all-important sound – the door, the telephone, a car – we can concentrate on nothing else and seem forgetful and stupid.

- Whisper lines 10–20. Leave a long listening pause at the end of line 16 and start of line 20. One of you can make sound effects.
- All of you are Portia, straining to hear sounds from the Capitol. As you listen, whisper your suspicions, hopes and fears for what this moment means to your life.
- Gather Portia's thoughts into a poem, in which every line starts 'Listen. In the wind I hear . . .'.

2 The power of the Soothsayer (in pairs)

a Think of a short but dramatic 'human interest' story you remember from the news. Talk together about how it would have been if a soothsayer had told the people what was to happen. Work the resulting story up into an improvisation. Try to make your soothsayer a character we can believe in today.

b Act out lines 21–46, thinking hard about why Portia nearly faints when she has talked to the Soothsayer. Does the Soothsayer recognise Portia as the wife of one of the conspirators?

c Write a short paragraph on the role of the Soothsayer in this scene. Consider everything he says about Caesar (e.g. 'I shall beseech him to befriend himself'). How fearful is he of what might happen?

d Write notes for the actor playing the Soothsayer about how to deliver his lines in this scene. What actions or gestures should accompany his words?

---

press to him   crowd round him
rumour   tumult, confusion
fray   battle
Sooth   truly
suit   petition

chance   happen
more void   more empty
merry   in good spirits
severally   in different directions

PORTIA Yes, bring me word, boy, if thy lord look well,
        For he went sickly forth, and take good note
        What Caesar doth, what suitors press to him.   15
        Hark, boy, what noise is that?
LUCIUS I hear none, madam.
PORTIA   Prithee listen well:
        I heard a bustling rumour, like a fray,
        And the wind brings it from the Capitol.
LUCIUS Sooth, madam, I hear nothing.   20

Enter the SOOTHSAYER

PORTIA Come hither, fellow, which way hast thou been?
SOOTHSAYER At mine own house, good lady.
PORTIA What is't o'clock?
SOOTHSAYER   About the ninth hour, lady.
PORTIA Is Caesar yet gone to the Capitol?
SOOTHSAYER Madam, not yet. I go to take my stand   25
        To see him pass on to the Capitol.
PORTIA Thou hast some suit to Caesar, hast thou not?
SOOTHSAYER That I have, lady, if it will please Caesar
        To be so good to Caesar as to hear me:
        I shall beseech him to befriend himself.   30
PORTIA Why, know'st thou any harm's intended towards him?
SOOTHSAYER None that I know will be, much that I fear may chance.
        Good morrow to you. Here the street is narrow:
        The throng that follows Caesar at the heels,
        Of senators, of praetors, common suitors,   35
        Will crowd a feeble man almost to death.
        I'll get me to a place more void, and there
        Speak to great Caesar as he comes along.   *Exit*
PORTIA I must go in. [*Aside*] Ay me, how weak a thing
        The heart of woman is! O Brutus,   40
        The heavens speed thee in thine enterprise!
        Sure the boy heard me. Brutus hath a suit
        That Caesar will not grant. O, I grow faint. –
        Run, Lucius, and commend me to my lord,
        Say I am merry. Come to me again   45
        And bring me word what he doth say to thee.
                      Exeunt [*severally*]

Looking back at Act 2
Activities for groups or individuals

1 Loyalties

In Scene 1 Brutus' loyalty is divided between Caesar, Cassius, Portia and himself. Work in four groups, each taking responsibility for one of these characters. Each group prepares the case for why its character has a strong claim on Brutus' loyalty. After your preparation is complete, the groups join together. Each group has one minute to present its case beginning: 'You owe me loyalty because . . .'.

Which character can make the strongest case?

2 The world through whose eyes?

Identify who you think is the major character in each of the four scenes in Act 2. Write a sentence for each saying what they think about the events unfolding in Rome.

3 Location, location, location

There are three very different settings used in Act 2. Brutus' orchard gives way to Caesar's home and then the action moves to the Roman streets.

Sketch your designs for a set that could quickly and effectively transform to each of these locations.

4 A female perspective . . .

Act 2 is the only one to give a real insight into the domestic lives of Portia and Calpurnia. Imagine that you work for a local radio station. You are researching a programme on the lifestyles of important Roman wives and you have arranged an interview with the two women. Script their contributions, making clear their attitudes to their husbands.

5 . . . and a male perspective

For a later programme you plan to focus on the home lives of Brutus and Caesar. Write their interview responses. Compare the men's accounts to the women's.

6 Lucius and Artemidorus: two small but crucial roles

Look back through Act 2 Scene 3 (Artemidorus) and Scene 4 (Lucius) for the contributions of these two minor characters. Match these photographs to lines in the script and then justify the inclusion of the two roles in the play.

Caesar ignores attempted warnings. Cassius misinterprets a senator's good wishes. Brutus reassures him. Trebonius draws Antony away.

1 Caesar enters the Capitol

At least fifteen characters enter to the sound of trumpets. Where might Shakespeare have moved each (bear in mind the change from street to Capitol at line 12)? Make an enlarged sketch of the Globe Theatre. On it, work out where everyone is at line 18. (For a description of Caesar's walk to the Capitol read Act 2 Scene 4, lines 34–6.)

2 What is your picture of Caesar? (in groups of three)

Caesar's words in lines 1–26 can be delivered in different ways in order to signal key aspects of his character moments before his death. Some critics see line 8 as pivotal. How does Caesar ignore Artemidorus here? Try different readings of lines 1, 8 and 10, then settle on the versions that work best. Present them to other groups and explain your choices.

3 With the benefit of hindsight (in pairs)

Some politicians can read the progress of friends and enemies by watching their behaviour outside the debating chamber and in session.

Read up to line 76 and see if there were warning signs that an assassination attempt was being made. Talk over the events as if you are the senators. Use your imagination to fill in the details.

---

schedule paper, document
touches concerns
Sirrah, give place get out of the way, man

makes to moves towards
sudden quick
turn back come back alive
be constant keep your nerve

Act 3 Scene 1
Rome The Capitol

Flourish. Enter CAESAR, BRUTUS, CASSIUS, CASCA, DECIUS,
  METELLUS, TREBONIUS, CINNA, ANTONY, Lepidus,
  ARTEMIDORUS, PUBLIUS, [POPILLIUS, Ligarius,] and the
  SOOTHSAYER

CAESAR The Ides of March are come.
SOOTHSAYER Ay, Caesar, but not gone.
ARTEMIDORUS Hail, Caesar! Read this schedule.
DECIUS Trebonius doth desire you to o'er-read
    (At your best leisure) this his humble suit.   5
ARTEMIDORUS O Caesar, read mine first, for mine's a suit
    That touches Caesar nearer. Read it, great Caesar.
CAESAR What touches us ourself shall be last served.
ARTEMIDORUS Delay not, Caesar, read it instantly.
CAESAR What, is the fellow mad?
PUBLIUS   Sirrah, give place.   10
CASSIUS What, urge you your petitions in the street?
    Come to the Capitol.
        [*Caesar enters the Capitol, the rest following*]
POPILLIUS I wish your enterprise today may thrive.
CASSIUS What enterprise, Popillius?
POPILLIUS   Fare you well.
        [*Leaves him and joins Caesar*]
BRUTUS What said Popillius Lena?   15
CASSIUS He wished today our enterprise might thrive.
    I fear our purpose is discoverèd.
BRUTUS Look how he makes to Caesar, mark him.
CASSIUS Casca, be sudden, for we fear prevention.
    Brutus, what shall be done? If this be known   20
    Cassius or Caesar never shall turn back,
    For I will slay myself.
BRUTUS   Cassius, be constant.
    Popillius Lena speaks not of our purposes,
    For look he smiles, and Caesar doth not change.
CASSIUS Trebonius knows his time, for look you, Brutus,   25
    He draws Mark Antony out of the way.
        [*Exeunt Antony and Trebonius*]

Repeal my brother's banishment, Metellus begs Caesar. Brutus and Cassius support him and get nearer to Caesar. Caesar adamantly refuses them all.

1 Focus on Caesar's behaviour (in groups of four)

In quick succession read Metellus Cimber's speech at line 33, Brutus' speech at line 52 (with Caesar's response) and Cassius' speech at line 55. Do this several times, giving everyone the chance to be Caesar.

Now look closely at Caesar's two long speeches (at lines 35 and 58) and talk together about how well he copes with the three senators' successive pleas to repeal Publius Cimber's banishment.

2 Caesar – 'constant as the northern star'

In refusing to repeal Publius Cimber's banishment, Caesar reacts like a tyrant whose will is fixed and unchangeable. How does this suit the conspirators' intentions?

Describe your impressions of this Caesar (from the 1983 RSC production) just before he is stabbed to death.

---

presently prefer immediately offer
addressed ready to begin
puissant powerful
couchings bowings down
turn preordinance . . . children make a children's game of long-established laws

Be not fond be not so foolish as
repealing recall from banishment
enfranchisement release (from banishment)
resting unchanging
firmament sky

DECIUS Where is Metellus Cimber? Let him go
    And presently prefer his suit to Caesar.
BRUTUS He is addressed, press near and second him.
CINNA Casca, you are the first that rears your hand.   30
CAESAR Are we all ready? What is now amiss
    That Caesar and his Senate must redress?
METELLUS Most high, most mighty, and most puissant Caesar,
    Metellus Cimber throws before thy seat
    An humble heart.
CAESAR   I must prevent thee, Cimber.   35
    These couchings and these lowly courtesies
    Might fire the blood of ordinary men
    And turn preordinance and first decree
    Into the law of children. Be not fond
    To think that Caesar bears such rebel blood   40
    That will be thawed from the true quality
    With that which melteth fools – I mean sweet words,
    Low-crookèd curtsies, and base spaniel fawning.
    Thy brother by decree is banishèd:
    If thou dost bend, and pray, and fawn for him,   45
    I spurn thee like a cur out of my way.
    Know Caesar doth not wrong, nor without cause
    Will he be satisfied.
METELLUS Is there no voice more worthy than my own
    To sound more sweetly in great Caesar's ear   50
    For the repealing of my banished brother?
BRUTUS I kiss thy hand, but not in flattery, Caesar,
    Desiring thee that Publius Cimber may
    Have an immediate freedom of repeal.
CAESAR What, Brutus?
CASSIUS   Pardon, Caesar! Caesar, pardon!   55
    As low as to thy foot doth Cassius fall
    To beg enfranchisement for Publius Cimber.
CAESAR I could be well moved, if I were as you;
    If I could pray to move, prayers would move me.
    But I am constant as the northern star,   60
    Of whose true-fixed and resting quality
    There is no fellow in the firmament.

Having declared himself the world's only constant man, Caesar is stabbed to death. Brutus tries to reassure all who flee, but the conspirators are left alone in the Senate.

---

1 The assassination (in groups of seven)

Brutus said, 'Let's be sacrificers, but not butchers' (Act 2 Scene 1, line 166), but the conspirators probably kill Caesar in different ways. Each person chooses which conspirator to play. Think about which part of Caesar's body he might choose to stab, and the style in which he would stab. Notice that Brutus is the last to attack.

Carefully stage the assassination. Then, without words, present it to the class in slow motion.

2 Caesar's final moment (in pairs)

Caesar's death line '*Et tu, Brute?* – Then fall, Caesar!' suggests Caesar's bewilderment at what is happening. Literally translated, the first three words mean 'Even you, Brutus?' Some argue that his friend's betrayal is as mortally wounding as Brutus' blade.

Take turns to create a 'snapshot' of Caesar at the moment of his death. Concentrate on facial expression and gesture. Hold your pose for a few seconds for your partner to look at.

3 What does Publius think? (in groups of four)

Publius, an old senator, speaks only once in this scene (at line 10). He silently witnesses the assassination of his leader and is dumbstruck at the turn of events. Brutus is concerned that Publius is 'affrighted' and tries to reassure him that no harm is intended to him.

Imagine that you are Publius. As the conspirators usher you away, you reflect on the amazing events that have just unfolded. How will you respond to the assassins' chant: 'Liberty! Freedom! Tyranny is dead!'? Express your thoughts.

---

apprehensive   quick to learn
holds . . . rank   keeps to his
  position
Olympus   the Greek mountain
  home of the gods
bootless   in vain, without effect

common pulpits   public speaking
  platforms
mutiny   uproar, confusion
Stand fast together   get ready to
  defend ourselves
abide   pay the penalty for

The skies are painted with unnumbered sparks,
They are all fire, and every one doth shine;
But there's but one in all doth hold his place. 65
So in the world: 'tis furnished well with men,
And men are flesh and blood, and apprehensive;
Yet in the number I do know but one
That unassailable holds on his rank,
Unshaked of motion, and that I am he 70
Let me a little show it, even in this:
That I was constant Cimber should be banished,
And constant do remain to keep him so.

CINNA O Caesar –

CAESAR   Hence! Wilt thou lift up Olympus?

DECIUS Great Caesar –

CAESAR   Doth not Brutus bootless kneel? 75

CASCA Speak hands for me!

They stab Caesar

CAESAR *Et tu, Brute?* – Then fall, Caesar!   *Dies*

CINNA Liberty! Freedom! Tyranny is dead!
          Run hence, proclaim, cry it about the streets.

CASSIUS Some to the common pulpits, and cry out, 80
          'Liberty, freedom, and enfranchisement!'

BRUTUS People and senators, be not affrighted,
          Fly not, stand still! Ambition's debt is paid.

CASCA Go to the pulpit, Brutus.

DECIUS   And Cassius too.

BRUTUS Where's Publius? 85

CINNA Here, quite confounded with this mutiny.

METELLUS Stand fast together lest some friend of Caesar's
          Should chance –

BRUTUS Talk not of standing. Publius, good cheer,
          There is no harm intended to your person, 90
          Nor to no Roman else. So tell them, Publius.

CASSIUS And leave us, Publius, lest that the people,
          Rushing on us, should do your age some mischief.

BRUTUS Do so, and let no man abide this deed
          But we the doers. 95

          [*Exeunt all but the conspirators*]

Trebonius reports panic outside. The conspirators prepare to depart to proclaim themselves liberators, their daggers and forearms ritually bloodied. They halt as Antony's servant enters, bringing his master's message.

1 'Let us bathe our hands in Caesar's blood'

This is how the 1980 Barbican production staged the moments following Caesar's assassination. Talk together about the different thoughts and emotions that these actors seem to feel as they stoop to smear their hands and weapons in Caesar's blood. How many of them appear excited by Brutus' proclamation that their actions have brought 'Peace, freedom, and liberty!'?

amazed utterly confounded
doomsday the Day of Judgement
drawing days out prolonging life
stand upon attach importance to
abridged shortened
in sport as entertainment

on Pompey's basis at the foot of Pompey's statue
knot group
Soft wait a minute
honest honourable

Enter TREBONIUS

CASSIUS Where is Antony?
TREBONIUS   Fled to his house amazed.
     Men, wives, and children stare, cry out, and run
     As it were doomsday.
BRUTUS   Fates, we will know your pleasures.
     That we shall die we know: 'tis but the time,
     And drawing days out, that men stand upon.   100
CASCA Why, he that cuts off twenty years of life
     Cuts off so many years of fearing death.
BRUTUS Grant that, and then is death a benefit.
     So are we Caesar's friends, that have abridged
     His time of fearing death. Stoop, Romans, stoop,   105
     And let us bathe our hands in Caesar's blood
     Up to the elbows and besmear our swords.
     Then walk we forth, even to the market-place,
     And waving our red weapons o'er our heads
     Let's all cry, 'Peace, freedom, and liberty!'   110
CASSIUS Stoop then and wash. How many ages hence
     Shall this our lofty scene be acted over
     In states unborn and accents yet unknown!
BRUTUS How many times shall Caesar bleed in sport,
     That now on Pompey's basis lies along   115
     No worthier than the dust!
CASSIUS   So oft as that shall be,
     So often shall the knot of us be called
     The men that gave their country liberty.
DECIUS What, shall we forth?
CASSIUS   Ay, every man away.
     Brutus shall lead, and we will grace his heels   120
     With the most boldest and best hearts of Rome.

Enter a SERVANT

BRUTUS Soft, who comes here? A friend of Antony's.
SERVANT Thus, Brutus, did my master bid me kneel,
     Thus did Mark Antony bid me fall down,
     And, being prostrate, thus he bade me say: 125
     Brutus is noble, wise, valiant, and honest;
     Caesar was mighty, bold, royal, and loving.

Antony's servant says that if Brutus' reasons for murder are convincing, Antony will follow Brutus. Brutus grants safe access to Antony, who enters and offers to be killed with Caesar.

---

1 Mark Antony – trustworthy or treacherous? (in pairs)

Cassius says before Mark Antony's entry: 'my misgiving still / Falls shrewdly to the purpose.' His suspicions turn out to be well founded. Hold a secret conversation with a fellow conspirator, in which you try to find reasons for Cassius' continuing suspicion. Analyse the servant's speech (lines 123–37) closely for deliberately vague or misleading phrases, especially about Brutus and Caesar.

2 Antony – a lesson in sincerity? (in small groups)

Antony confronts Caesar's killers while their hands are still covered in his blood (Shakespeare departed from his source material to include this moment). He is quick to declare his reverence for Caesar . . . and to suggest that he would willingly die alongside his former leader. But is he telling the truth?

- How would you have Antony enter after line 146? Brutus is keen to welcome him. How does Antony respond?
- One of you reads Antony's lines 148–63, emphasising all references to blood and death. The others, as blood-soaked assassins, listen closely to his words. Afterwards, the group talks together about the emotive qualities of Antony's speech. Is Antony speaking from the heart, or does he want to make the conspirators squirm . . . or both? Discuss your ideas and collect evidence to justify your conclusions.

---

this untrod state these unprecedented circumstances
presently at once
my misgiving . . . purpose my suspicions always turn out to be close to the truth
measure extent, size

rank rotten or diseased
bear me hard hate me
purpled Antony says Caesar's blood is the colour of royalty
apt to die ready, willing to die
mean of death way of dying

Say I love Brutus, and I honour him;
Say I feared Caesar, honoured him, and loved him.
If Brutus will vouchsafe that Antony   130
May safely come to him and be resolved
How Caesar hath deserved to lie in death,
Mark Antony shall not love Caesar dead
So well as Brutus living, but will follow
The fortunes and affairs of noble Brutus   135
Through the hazards of this untrod state
With all true faith. So says my master Antony.

BRUTUS Thy master is a wise and valiant Roman,
I never thought him worse.
Tell him, so please him come unto this place,   140
He shall be satisfied and by my honour
Depart untouched.

SERVANT   I'll fetch him presently.   *Exit Servant*

BRUTUS I know that we shall have him well to friend.

CASSIUS I wish we may. But yet have I a mind
That fears him much, and my misgiving still   145
Falls shrewdly to the purpose.

Enter ANTONY

BRUTUS But here comes Antony. Welcome, Mark Antony!

ANTONY O mighty Caesar! Dost thou lie so low?
Are all thy conquests, glories, triumphs, spoils
Shrunk to this little measure? Fare thee well!   150
I know not, gentlemen, what you intend,
Who else must be let blood, who else is rank.
If I myself, there is no hour so fit
As Caesar's death's hour, nor no instrument
Of half that worth as those your swords made rich   155
With the most noble blood of all this world.
I do beseech ye, if you bear me hard,
Now, whilst your purpled hands do reek and smoke,
Fulfil your pleasure. Live a thousand years,
I shall not find myself so apt to die: 160
No place will please me so, no mean of death,
As here by Caesar, and by you cut off,
The choice and master spirits of this age.

Brutus claims that pity for Rome killed Caesar. Brutus loves Antony and loved Caesar. Antony shakes the conspirators' hands, but fears this act of friendship wrongs Caesar.

1 Brutus and Cassius – two different politicians (in pairs)

One of you reads Brutus' lines 164–76; the other takes Cassius' lines 177–8. Then talk together about how differently the two conspirators treat Antony. Make a list of the contrasting points that emerge.

2 Outward action, secret thoughts (in eight pairs)

At the end of Act 3 Scene 1 we have no doubt about Antony's intentions towards the conspirators, however he behaves towards them here.

Work up a presentation of lines 184–9 in which each character is played by two people. One speaks and behaves as in the scripted action (the *action* player), the other utters secret unscripted thoughts (the *thought* player). When the thought player stamps a foot, the action freezes while thoughts are spoken. Action resumes with another stamp from the thought player. Thought players shadow action players during presentation. Each bloody handshake is a cue for a second thought from Antony or a conspirator – or both!

Before presentation, action and thought players research the script together to find what their character may think of Antony, or he of them. During presentation, thought players can improvise or read from notes, but always with appropriate expression and tone of voice – which may be quite different from those of the action player!

3 Conspirators – the facts (in groups of three to five)

Apart from Brutus and Cassius, we shall not see the seven conspirators again. You and your team of reporters have to profile the involvement of each one in the assassination. Give news-hungry Rome a quick character sketch (perhaps with pictures) of the men behind the words and the daggers.

---

leaden points (i.e. soft and harmless)
Our arms ... do receive you in we welcome you like a brother despite our savage appearance
voice vote, influence
dignities positions of influence

credit honour, reputation
conceit me think of me
corse corpse
close / In terms of friendship make a deal

BRUTUS O Antony, beg not your death of us.
    Though now we must appear bloody and cruel,   165
    As by our hands and this our present act
    You see we do, yet see you but our hands
    And this the bleeding business they have done.
    Our hearts you see not, they are pitiful;
    And pity to the general wrong of Rome –   170
    As fire drives out fire, so pity pity –
    Hath done this deed on Caesar. For your part,
    To you our swords have leaden points, Mark Antony;
    Our arms in strength of malice, and our hearts
    Of brothers' temper, do receive you in   175
    With all kind love, good thoughts, and reverence.
CASSIUS Your voice shall be as strong as any man's
    In the disposing of new dignities.
BRUTUS Only be patient till we have appeased
    The multitude, beside themselves with fear,   180
    And then we will deliver you the cause
    Why I, that did love Caesar when I struck him,
    Have thus proceeded.
ANTONY   I doubt not of your wisdom.
    Let each man render me his bloody hand.
    First, Marcus Brutus, will I shake with you;   185
    Next, Caius Cassius, do I take your hand;
    Now, Decius Brutus, yours; now yours, Metellus;
    Yours, Cinna; and, my valiant Casca, yours;
    Though last, not least in love, yours, good Trebonius.
    Gentlemen all – alas, what shall I say?   190
    My credit now stands on such slippery ground
    That one of two bad ways you must conceit me,
    Either a coward or a flatterer.
    That I did love thee, Caesar, O, 'tis true.
    If then thy spirit look upon us now,   195
    Shall it not grieve thee dearer than thy death
    To see thy Antony making his peace,
    Shaking the bloody fingers of thy foes –
    Most noble – in the presence of thy corse?
    Had I as many eyes as thou hast wounds,   200
    Weeping as fast as they stream forth thy blood,
    It would become me better than to close
    In terms of friendship with thine enemies.

Antony praises Caesar. Cassius asks if Antony intends to show friendship to the conspirators. Yes, replies Antony, if reasons for Caesar's death are given. Cassius is uneasy about Antony speaking at Caesar's funeral.

1 'That I did love thee, Caesar' (in small groups)

Even though the conspirators look on, Antony is effusive in declaring his love for Caesar. Work through lines 194–210. Antony's words resonate with two image patterns: blood and hunting. Caesar's wounds are like eyes that weep with blood; Caesar the man is described as a hunted animal (a 'hart' is a deer, but it is also a clever pun suggesting the word 'heart' to his audience).

Talk together about what you think Antony's intentions are in speaking as he does in lines 194–210.

2 Brutus gives Antony satisfaction (in groups of four)

Antony asks the conspirators to 'give me reasons / Why and wherein Caesar was dangerous' (lines 221–2). But Brutus never does explain his actions to Antony. Hold the conversation they might have had, joined by Octavius and Cassius.

3 Antony – one final request (in pairs)

A crucial moment. In lines 227–30, Antony requests that he be allowed to 'Produce his [Caesar's] body to the market-place' and speak like a 'friend' at his funeral. This provokes differing responses in Brutus and Cassius. Cassius urgently takes Brutus aside at line 231 to talk in confidence with him.

Take parts and read Brutus and Cassius' brief private conversation (lines 231–43). Afterwards, talk about what the lines reveal of the two men's characters.

---

bayed   hunted and cornered
hart   see Activity 1 above
Signed in thy spoil   marked with bits of your flesh and blood

Lethe   river of the underworld
cold modesty   being very restrained
pricked   marked down, listed
in the order   as part of

Pardon me, Julius! Here wast thou bayed, brave hart,
Here didst thou fall, and here thy hunters stand, 205
Signed in thy spoil and crimsoned in thy Lethe.
O world! Thou wast the forest to this hart,
And this indeed, O world, the heart of thee.
How like a deer strucken by many princes
Dost thou here lie! 210

CASSIUS Mark Antony –

ANTONY   Pardon me, Caius Cassius,
The enemies of Caesar shall say this;
Then, in a friend, it is cold modesty.

CASSIUS I blame you not for praising Caesar so,
But what compact mean you to have with us? 215
Will you be pricked in number of our friends,
Or shall we on and not depend on you?

ANTONY Therefore I took your hands, but was indeed
Swayed from the point by looking down on Caesar.
Friends am I with you all, and love you all, 220
Upon this hope, that you shall give me reasons
Why and wherein Caesar was dangerous.

BRUTUS Or else were this a savage spectacle.
Our reasons are so full of good regard
That were you, Antony, the son of Caesar 225
You should be satisfied.

ANTONY   That's all I seek,
And am, moreover, suitor that I may
Produce his body to the market-place,
And in the pulpit, as becomes a friend,
Speak in the order of his funeral. 230

BRUTUS You shall, Mark Antony.

CASSIUS   Brutus, a word with you.
[*Aside to Brutus*] You know not what you do. Do not consent
That Antony speak in his funeral.
Know you how much the people may be moved
By that which he will utter?

BRUTUS [*Aside to Cassius*]   By your pardon, 235
I will myself into the pulpit first
And show the reason of our Caesar's death.

Antony is given permission to speak at Caesar's funeral after Brutus, but not to blame the conspirators. Left alone with Caesar's body, Antony prophesies horrific civil war.

---

1 'O, pardon me, thou bleeding piece of earth'

It is worth exploring the dramatic impact of Antony's crucial soliloquy, spoken over the mutilated body of his friend.

a Antony's public and private thoughts (in pairs)

Cassius' suspicions about the potential threat posed by Antony prove correct. Now alone, he reveals his true feelings about Caesar's murder and the men who killed him.

Share out the lines and read through Antony's soliloquy (lines 254–75). Find words in it that convey what Antony truly feels about a) Caesar, b) his murderers and c) revenge. Write them down.

Now look back through the earlier part of the scene, starting at Antony's entrance after line 146. Compare his 'soliloquy' thoughts and feelings with those he speaks openly to the conspirators. In what ways are they similar and why? In what ways are they very different?

b Nightmare voices (in groups of five or more)

Work out how you can present Antony's soliloquy to create the maximum horror. Use all your voices, sometimes speaking together, sometimes separately or individually. You can repeat or echo words, emphasise sound patterns and rhythms, build to a crescendo, fade to nothing, be suddenly loud, suddenly soft. No need to stick to words; you can make rhythmic, threatening noises or other sounds which the words suggest. By putting people in different parts of the room you can get quadraphonic sound.

You may find you know the speech by heart after all this work!

---

protest proclaim
advantage do (us) good
fall happen
tide of times changing course of history
cumber trouble or load down
quartered cut to pieces

choked . . . fell deeds hardened to seeing acts of cruelty
Ate goddess of revenge
havoc (the signal in war for total slaughter)
carrion men rotting corpses

What Antony shall speak, I will protest
He speaks by leave and by permission,
And that we are contented Caesar shall   240
Have all true rites and lawful ceremonies.
It shall advantage more than do us wrong.
CASSIUS [*Aside to Brutus*] I know not what may fall, I like it not.
BRUTUS Mark Antony, here take you Caesar's body.
You shall not in your funeral speech blame us,   245
But speak all good you can devise of Caesar
And say you do't by our permission,
Else shall you not have any hand at all
About his funeral. And you shall speak
In the same pulpit whereto I am going,   250
After my speech is ended.
ANTONY   Be it so,
I do desire no more.
BRUTUS Prepare the body then and follow us.
                              Exeunt [all but] Antony
ANTONY O, pardon me, thou bleeding piece of earth,
That I am meek and gentle with these butchers!   255
Thou art the ruins of the noblest man
That ever livèd in the tide of times.
Woe to the hand that shed this costly blood!
Over thy wounds now do I prophesy –
Which like dumb mouths do ope their ruby lips   260
To beg the voice and utterance of my tongue –
A curse shall light upon the limbs of men:
Domestic fury and fierce civil strife
Shall cumber all the parts of Italy;
Blood and destruction shall be so in use   265
And dreadful objects so familiar
That mothers shall but smile when they behold
Their infants quartered with the hands of war,
All pity choked with custom of fell deeds;
And Caesar's spirit, ranging for revenge,   270
With Ate by his side come hot from hell,
Shall in these confines with a monarch's voice
Cry havoc and let slip the dogs of war,
That this foul deed shall smell above the earth
With carrion men groaning for burial.   275

Octavius' servant reports his master's approach. Antony suggests that Octavius waits until the people's mood has been tested. In the market-place, Brutus and Cassius prepare to speak.

---

1 The day that Caesar was killed (in groups of three to six)

Many adults remember the exact time and place they heard of President John F. Kennedy's assassination in 1963. Imagine how ordinary Romans might have felt on hearing of Caesar's death. Write a report to send to Octavius Caesar (Julius Caesar's nephew and heir) about the mood of the city after the assassination. Begin with Antony's words at line 288: 'Here is a mourning Rome, a dangerous Rome'.

2 Great speeches in the mouth and in the ear (in groups of four to six)

Some of the greatest oratory (public speaking) that Shakespeare wrote is in Act 3 Scene 2. Brutus' and Mark Antony's speeches (lines 13–39 and lines 65–242) have to be read aloud *and listened to* in their entirety for their art to be fully appreciated.

Two or three of you read the speeches aloud, taking a sentence each in turn while the rest listen closely *without following the script*. Leave out the Plebeians' lines. Then swap over. After each speech, discuss how it felt when you spoke it and how it felt when you listened to it.

3 Cassius' speech to the people

At line 10 of Act 3 Scene 2 Cassius leaves to speak to half the crowd in another street. Look back at how Cassius speaks in Act 1 Scenes 2 and 3 and write the speech he might have delivered to the crowd. The Elizabethan lesson in rhetoric on page 92 will help you. You could also look at the ways in which Brutus (line 13) and Antony (line 65) begin their speeches to the crowd in this scene.

Your class could be the crowd to whom you deliver the speech, who will no doubt have questions that they want answered.

Octavius Caesar see Activity 1 above
Passion intense emotion
seven leagues about twenty-one miles
Post back hurry back

Hie hence get you gone
try discover
take / The cruel issue react to the savage actions
PLEBEIANS ordinary people, workers

Enter Octavio's SERVANT

You serve Octavius Caesar, do you not?

SERVANT I do, Mark Antony.

ANTONY Caesar did write for him to come to Rome.

SERVANT He did receive his letters, and is coming,
And bid me say to you by word of mouth –   280
[Seeing the body]
O Caesar!

ANTONY Thy heart is big, get thee apart and weep.
Passion, I see, is catching, for mine eyes,
Seeing those beads of sorrow stand in thine,
Began to water. Is thy master coming?   285

SERVANT He lies tonight within seven leagues of Rome.

ANTONY Post back with speed and tell him what hath chanced.
Here is a mourning Rome, a dangerous Rome,
No Rome of safety for Octavius yet:
Hie hence and tell him so. Yet stay awhile,   290
Thou shalt not back till I have borne this corse
Into the market-place. There shall I try
In my oration how the people take
The cruel issue of these bloody men,
According to the which thou shalt discourse   295
To young Octavius of the state of things.
Lend me your hand.
                                Exeunt [with Caesar's body]

Act 3 Scene 2
Rome The market-place

Enter BRUTUS *and Cassius with the* PLEBEIANS

ALL We will be satisfied! Let us be satisfied!

BRUTUS Then follow me and give me audience, friends.
Cassius, go you into the other street
And part the numbers.
Those that will hear me speak, let 'em stay here;   5

Brutus addresses the people. He says he loved Rome's freedom more than Caesar. The crowd accepts it. Antony enters with Caesar's corpse.

1 An Elizabethan lesson in rhetoric (in groups of three)

'Rhetoric' is the art of public speaking and debate. An Elizabethan text-book on rhetoric would typically divide up a speech like this:

exordium (introduction) to gain the attention and approval of the hearers

narratio (development) so that listeners may fully understand the matter being discussed

confirmatio (evidence) proofs, arguments and reasons, illustrated by quotations

confutatio (dealing with objections) consideration of what objections may be raised and how to answer them

conclusio (summing up) a short recapitulation of the main point(s).

a Find these five sections in lines 13–39 of Brutus' speech (they are very clear) and lines 65–242 of Antony's (perhaps less clear). Try reading out loud one of Brutus' sections, then the corresponding one of Antony. Note contrasts in technique, thought and behaviour.

b Identify, and comment upon, any other persuasive techniques Brutus uses in his speech – for example repetitions and echoes, balanced sentences, rhetorical questions and flattering his audience. How do you respond? Are you persuaded?

2 Enter Mark Antony with Caesar's body

Antony likes plays and, in Act 3 Scene 1, demonstrates what a good actor he is himself! Imagine you are Antony, and plan your big entry with Caesar's corpse. Think carefully about: your own appearance (blood?); how you relate to the corpse; the corpse itself and its presentation ('coffin' at line 98?); and finally where to enter and where to stand while Brutus speaks. You could write notes for yourself to guide your actions.

---

severally separately
lovers/lover dear friend(s)
have respect . . . honour bear in mind I am a man of honour
Censure me judge me
base lowborn

rude ignorant, uncivilised
The question of the facts of
enrolled recorded
extenuated played down
enforced heavily emphasised

Those that will follow Cassius, go with him;
And public reasons shall be renderèd
Of Caesar's death.

1 PLEBEIAN   I will hear Brutus speak.
2 PLEBEIAN I will hear Cassius and compare their reasons
      When severally we hear them renderèd.   10
              [*Exit Cassius with some of the Plebeians*]
              [*Brutus goes into the pulpit*]
3 PLEBEIAN The noble Brutus is ascended, silence!
BRUTUS Be patient till the last.
      Romans, countrymen, and lovers, hear me for my cause, and be silent
      that you may hear. Believe me for mine honour, and have respect to
      mine honour that you may believe. Censure me in your wisdom, and   15
      awake your senses that you may the better judge. If there be any in this
      assembly, any dear friend of Caesar's, to him I say that Brutus' love to
      Caesar was no less than his. If then that friend demand why Brutus
      rose against Caesar, this is my answer: not that I loved Caesar less,
      but that I loved Rome more. Had you rather Caesar were living, and   20
      die all slaves, than that Caesar were dead, to live all freemen? As
      Caesar loved me, I weep for him; as he was fortunate, I rejoice at it; as
      he was valiant, I honour him; but, as he was ambitious, I slew him.
      There is tears for his love, joy for his fortune, honour for his valour,
      and death for his ambition. Who is here so base that would be a   25
      bondman? If any, speak, for him have I offended. Who is here so rude
      that would not be a Roman? If any, speak, for him have I offended.
      Who is here so vile that will not love his country? If any, speak, for him
      have I offended. I pause for a reply.
ALL None, Brutus, none.   30
BRUTUS Then none have I offended. I have done no more to Caesar than
      you shall do to Brutus. The question of his death is enrolled in the
      Capitol, his glory not extenuated wherein he was worthy, nor his
      offences enforced for which he suffered death.

      Enter MARK ANTONY [*and others*] *with Caesar's body*

      Here comes his body, mourned by Mark Antony, who, though he had   35
      no hand in his death, shall receive the benefit of his dying, a place in
      the commonwealth, as which of you shall not? With this I depart: that,
      as I slew my best lover for the good of Rome, I have the same dagger
      for myself when it shall please my country to need my death.
              [*Comes down*]

Hailed as a new leader, Brutus asks the crowd to hear Antony out. In the pulpit, Antony at first seems to reflect the anti-Caesar mood of the crowd.

---

1 Antony takes centre stage (in groups of six)

Brutus descends from the pulpit to a hero's reception from the crowd. The third Plebeian even shouts, 'Let him be Caesar'! Brutus' gracious departure paves the way for Antony's address. But before Antony can begin his funeral oration, he must subdue the raucous, pro-Brutus crowd.

Take parts (you will need four Plebeians, Brutus and Antony). Start at the moment when Brutus 'Comes down' from the speaker's platform. Read through all the lines until Antony begins his speech at line 65. Then work out how you would stage this scene. You will need to show how the mood of the Plebeians changes and how Antony gradually subdues them in order to begin his address. It would be good if you could learn some of the lines so that you can include dramatic action and gesture – and don't forget that Caesar's body is on stage!

2 The speaker's skill (whole class)

Antony, in his funeral oration (lines 65–99), uses many of the persuasive techniques that Brutus employed earlier. Amongst other strategies, he

- asks for his listeners' attention
- explains his purpose
- acknowledges and flatters Brutus
- praises Caesar
- shows his own distress.

a One person reads Antony's speech. The others line up on the opposite side of the room. Each time Antony uses one of the persuasive techniques listed, the others take a step towards him and call out the technique used.

b Between lines 65 and 151 of Antony's speech you will find five or six key words (such as ambition/ambitious) emphasised and repeated seven to fifteen times each. Find some of them and work out what effects the repetitions have.

Do grace to	show respect for	**beholding to**	grateful to
Tending to	concerning	**interrèd**	buried

ALL Live, Brutus, live, live!   40

1 PLEBEIAN Bring him with triumph home unto his house.

2 PLEBEIAN Give him a statue with his ancestors.

3 PLEBEIAN Let him be Caesar.

4 PLEBEIAN   Caesar's better parts
    Shall be crowned in Brutus.

1 PLEBEIAN   We'll bring him to his house
    With shouts and clamours.

BRUTUS   My countrymen –   45

2 PLEBEIAN Peace, silence, Brutus speaks!

1 PLEBEIAN   Peace ho!

BRUTUS Good countrymen, let me depart alone,
    And, for my sake, stay here with Antony.
    Do grace to Caesar's corpse, and grace his speech
    Tending to Caesar's glories, which Mark Antony   50
    (By our permission) is allowed to make.
    I do entreat you, not a man depart,
    Save I alone, till Antony have spoke.   *Exit*

1 PLEBEIAN Stay ho, and let us hear Mark Antony.

3 PLEBEIAN Let him go up into the public chair,   55
    We'll hear him. Noble Antony, go up.

ANTONY For Brutus' sake, I am beholding to you.
            [*Goes into the pulpit*]

4 PLEBEIAN What does he say of Brutus?

3 PLEBEIAN   He says for Brutus' sake
    He finds himself beholding to us all.

4 PLEBEIAN 'Twere best he speak no harm of Brutus here!   60

1 PLEBEIAN This Caesar was a tyrant.

3 PLEBEIAN   Nay, that's certain:
    We are blest that Rome is rid of him.

2 PLEBEIAN Peace, let us hear what Antony can say.

ANTONY You gentle Romans –

ALL   Peace ho, let us hear him.

ANTONY Friends, Romans, countrymen, lend me your ears!   65
    I come to bury Caesar, not to praise him.
    The evil that men do lives after them,
    The good is oft interrèd with their bones:
    So let it be with Caesar. The noble Brutus
    Hath told you Caesar was ambitious;   70
    If it were so, it was a grievous fault,
    And grievously hath Caesar answered it.

While appearing to agree with Brutus' portrait of Caesar, Antony rejects it in reality by listing Caesar's virtues. The crowd becomes uncertain, swayed by Antony's grief.

1 Mark Antony delivers his funeral oration in the 2001 RSC production

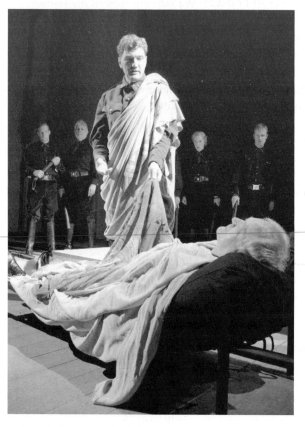

- Read through the whole of Antony's funeral speech (lines 65–251) and decide what line you think he is speaking here. Give your reasons.
- Compare this picture with the one on page 98. Which portrayal of Antony comes closer to your interpretation of the character? Give your reasons.

---

general coffers public finances
Lupercal festival of Lupercalia (the setting for Act 1 Scene 2; see p. 10 and **Lupercal**, p. 172)

disprove prove wrong, refute
judgement wisdom, good sense
dear abide it pay dearly for it

Here, under leave of Brutus and the rest –
For Brutus is an honourable man,
So are they all, all honourable men –   75
Come I to speak in Caesar's funeral.
He was my friend, faithful and just to me,
But Brutus says he was ambitious,
And Brutus is an honourable man.
He hath brought many captives home to Rome,   80
Whose ransoms did the general coffers fill;
Did this in Caesar seem ambitious?
When that the poor have cried, Caesar hath wept:
Ambition should be made of sterner stuff;
Yet Brutus says he was ambitious,   85
And Brutus is an honourable man.
You all did see that on the Lupercal
I thrice presented him a kingly crown,
Which he did thrice refuse. Was this ambition?
Yet Brutus says he was ambitious,   90
And sure he is an honourable man.
I speak not to disprove what Brutus spoke,
But here I am to speak what I do know.
You all did love him once, not without cause;
What cause withholds you then to mourn for him?   95
O judgement, thou art fled to brutish beasts,
And men have lost their reason! Bear with me,
My heart is in the coffin there with Caesar,
And I must pause till it come back to me.

1 PLEBEIAN   Methinks there is much reason in his sayings.   100
2 PLEBEIAN   If thou consider rightly of the matter,
Caesar has had great wrong.
3 PLEBEIAN   Has he, masters!
I fear there will a worse come in his place.
4 PLEBEIAN   Marked ye his words? He would not take the crown,
Therefore 'tis certain he was not ambitious.   105
1 PLEBEIAN   If it be found so, some will dear abide it.
2 PLEBEIAN   Poor soul, his eyes are red as fire with weeping.
3 PLEBEIAN   There's not a nobler man in Rome than Antony.
4 PLEBEIAN   Now mark him, he begins again to speak.

Antony pleads that the Plebeians must remain loyal to the conspirators, and that he must wrong Caesar by refusing to let them know how generous his will is to them. Read it! they shout.

1 Antony works the crowd

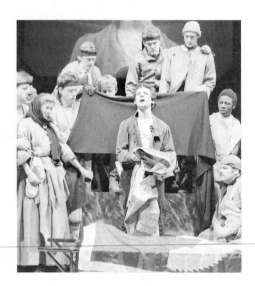

Describe the impact of Antony's words on the crowd in this 1983 RSC production.

2 'The will, the will, we will hear Caesar's will!' (in groups of four)

This is perhaps Antony's masterstroke. So skilled at focusing his listeners' attention on a specific detail, in line 120 he 'just happens to' mention Caesar's will. He very probably doesn't have Caesar's will at this point (he sends Lepidus to fetch the will from Caesar's house in Act 4 Scene 1, lines 7–9, having fled to his own house following the assassination), so this tactic is a con.

Take parts and act out lines 120–54. Concentrate on the techniques Antony uses to 'work' his audience. How does he tease them? What is the role of the fourth Plebeian? What is the mood of the crowd at this point? Why would Antony decide to leave the pulpit and join them?

---

mutiny   riot, disorder
closet   private room
commons   ordinary people
napkins   handkerchiefs

issue   children
o'ershot myself   gone further than I meant

ANTONY But yesterday the word of Caesar might   110
        Have stood against the world; now lies he there,
        And none so poor to do him reverence.
        O masters, if I were disposed to stir
        Your hearts and minds to mutiny and rage,
        I should do Brutus wrong and Cassius wrong,   115
        Who (you all know) are honourable men.
        I will not do them wrong; I rather choose
        To wrong the dead, to wrong myself and you,
        Than I will wrong such honourable men.
        But here's a parchment with the seal of Caesar,   120
        I found it in his closet, 'tis his will.
        Let but the commons hear this testament –
        Which, pardon me, I do not mean to read –
        And they would go and kiss dead Caesar's wounds
        And dip their napkins in his sacred blood,   125
        Yea, beg a hair of him for memory,
        And, dying, mention it within their wills,
        Bequeathing it as a rich legacy
        Unto their issue.
4 PLEBEIAN We'll hear the will. Read it, Mark Antony.   130
ALL The will, the will, we will hear Caesar's will!
ANTONY Have patience, gentle friends, I must not read it.
        It is not meet you know how Caesar loved you:
        You are not wood, you are not stones, but men,
        And, being men, hearing the will of Caesar,   135
        It will inflame you, it will make you mad.
        'Tis good you know not that you are his heirs,
        For if you should, O, what would come of it?
4 PLEBEIAN Read the will, we'll hear it, Antony.
        You shall read us the will, Caesar's will!   140
ANTONY Will you be patient? Will you stay awhile?
        I have o'ershot myself to tell you of it.
        I fear I wrong the honourable men
        Whose daggers have stabbed Caesar, I do fear it.
4 PLEBEIAN They were traitors. Honourable men!   145
ALL The will! The testament!
2 PLEBEIAN They were villains, murderers! The will, read the will!
ANTONY You will compel me then to read the will?

Obeying the crowd, Antony comes down to show them Caesar's corpse, starting with the dagger cuts in his cloak. The Plebeians weep.

---

1 How well does Antony manipulate his audience? (in groups of three or four)

Read Act 3 Scene 1 again closely, and write a precise and factual account of what actually happened when Caesar was murdered. Then compare it with Mark Antony's account in lines 160–80. What reason(s) can you give for being very dubious about the accuracy of Antony's description of the murder?

Just as a jury has to recognise the bias of both prosecuting and defending barristers in order to arrive at a fair verdict, see if you can spot how Antony colours his account to manipulate your emotions and show the conspirators in a bad light.

'Emotive language' is language that seeks to arouse powerful emotions such as fear, pity, anger and so on. Make a list of three or four of the most powerfully emotive words or phrases that Antony uses, explaining how and why you think they spark such strong responses in the people watching and listening to him.

2 The secret life of objects

Antony assembles the crowd around Caesar's body. Again, as on page 99, he concentrates on very specific physical details, this time Caesar's cloak. Previously worn at a famous military victory, it is now bloodied and gashed by the conspirators' daggers. And Caesar lies dead at the foot of Pompey's statue.

Choose either Caesar's cloak or Pompey's statue. Give it a history. Try to create a story behind each of its flaws and marks. Draw your object and write your ideas around the image.

---

far off further off
mantle cloak
Nervii a fierce tribe in Gaul (brilliantly defeated by Caesar)
envious malicious
As rushing out as if it were rushing out

unkindly savagely/unnaturally
most unkindest most savage / most unnatural
flourished waved its weapons in triumph
dint blow, force

Then make a ring about the corpse of Caesar
And let me show you him that made the will.   150
Shall I descend? And will you give me leave?
ALL Come down.
2 PLEBEIAN Descend.
3 PLEBEIAN You shall have leave.
                    [*Antony comes down from the pulpit*]
4 PLEBEIAN A ring, stand round.   155
1 PLEBEIAN Stand from the hearse, stand from the body.
2 PLEBEIAN Room for Antony, most noble Antony.
ANTONY Nay, press not so upon me, stand far off.
ALL Stand back! Room, bear back!
ANTONY If you have tears, prepare to shed them now.   160
You all do know this mantle. I remember
The first time ever Caesar put it on,
'Twas on a summer's evening, in his tent,
That day he overcame the Nervii.
Look, in this place ran Cassius' dagger through;   165
See what a rent the envious Casca made;
Through this the well-belovèd Brutus stabbed,
And as he plucked his cursèd steel away,
Mark how the blood of Caesar followed it,
As rushing out of doors to be resolved   170
If Brutus so unkindly knocked or no,
For Brutus, as you know, was Caesar's angel.
Judge, O you gods, how dearly Caesar loved him!
This was the most unkindest cut of all.
For when the noble Caesar saw him stab,   175
Ingratitude, more strong than traitors' arms,
Quite vanquished him. Then burst his mighty heart,
And, in his mantle muffling up his face,
Even at the base of Pompey's statue
(Which all the while ran blood) great Caesar fell.   180
O, what a fall was there, my countrymen!
Then I, and you, and all of us fell down,
Whilst bloody treason flourished over us.
O, now you weep, and I perceive you feel
The dint of pity. These are gracious drops.   185

There are cries of grief when Antony displays the body. When he cleverly praises Brutus' oratory over his own, the enraged crowd move to attack the conspirators.

---

1 Echoes in the market-place (in groups of four)

Antony finishes here with an explosion of verbal fireworks. Divide lines 214–20 between pairs, one playing Antony and the other an echo that picks up words and sounds which would reverberate through the market-place. Together, decide which words to emphasise for maximum effect. Finally, put the passage together and run through it as a group.

2 Blaming conspirators (in groups of four to five)

Brutus let Antony speak on the condition 'You shall not in your funeral speech blame us' (Act 3 Scene 1, line 245).

Imagine that by Scene 2, line 220, the conspirators have found out how Antony has roused the people, and send in a force to arrest him and disperse the crowd.

Organise your group into lawyers for the prosecution and the defence at Antony's trial. The prosecution must prove that he did blame the conspirators, the defence that he did not. Both sides must look very closely at the language of the speech.

When you have prepared your arguments, join up with another group, choose a judge, lawyers and a jury, and run the trial for fifteen minutes or so. Finally, get the jury to sift the evidence and arrive at a verdict.

3 Orators ancient and modern

You have now heard the oratory of Murellus, Cassius, Caesar, Brutus and Antony. Find ten typical lines from each and jot down your thoughts about their styles of speech-making.

As you study *Julius Caesar* further, watch public figures on television and see if they are like the orators in the play. You could even rewrite and deliver a speech from the play in the style and manner of a well-known modern-day speaker!

---

vesture clothing
marred . . . with ruined as you see by
About! Let's go looking!

private griefs personal grievances
ruffle up stir up to rage

Kind souls, what weep you when you but behold
Our Caesar's vesture wounded? Look you here,
Here is himself, marred as you see with traitors.

1 PLEBEIAN O piteous spectacle!

2 PLEBEIAN O noble Caesar!   190

3 PLEBEIAN O woeful day!

4 PLEBEIAN O traitors, villains!

1 PLEBEIAN O most bloody sight!

2 PLEBEIAN We will be revenged!

ALL Revenge! About! Seek! Burn! Fire! Kill!   195
      Slay! Let not a traitor live!

ANTONY Stay, countrymen.

1 PLEBEIAN Peace there, hear the noble Antony.

2 PLEBEIAN We'll hear him, we'll follow him, we'll die with him.

ANTONY Good friends, sweet friends, let me not stir you up   200
      To such a sudden flood of mutiny.
      They that have done this deed are honourable.
      What private griefs they have, alas, I know not,
      That made them do it. They are wise and honourable,
      And will no doubt with reasons answer you.   205
      I come not, friends, to steal away your hearts.
      I am no orator, as Brutus is,
      But – as you know me all – a plain blunt man
      That love my friend, and that they know full well
      That gave me public leave to speak of him.   210
      For I have neither wit, nor words, nor worth,
      Action, nor utterance, nor the power of speech
      To stir men's blood. I only speak right on.
      I tell you that which you yourselves do know,
      Show you sweet Caesar's wounds, poor, poor, dumb mouths, 215
      And bid them speak for me. But were I Brutus,
      And Brutus Antony, there were an Antony
      Would ruffle up your spirits and put a tongue
      In every wound of Caesar, that should move
      The stones of Rome to rise and mutiny.   220

ALL We'll mutiny.

1 PLEBEIAN   We'll burn the house of Brutus.

3 PLEBEIAN Away then, come, seek the conspirators.

Antony reveals how much Caesar's will left to the people. They swear vengeance on the conspirators and leave. Alone, Antony confides his satisfaction. Octavius' arrival is announced.

1 A Caesar memorial (individual or small group)

Design a striking and impressive layout or feature which will celebrate the life of your benefactor, Caesar. It is to be installed in his newly bequeathed gardens. Do not let your imagination be hindered by practicalities!

Work individually or in a group as a design consultancy. Present your ideas very fully worked out or as a series of sketches with explanation. Use the play to give you ideas: for example, Antony's funeral eulogies (Act 3 Scene 2), Calpurnia's dream (Act 2 Scene 2), even Cassius' reference to Caesar as Colossus, storm, fire, and so on (Act 1 Scenes 2 and 3).

2 'Mischief, thou art afoot'

In lines 250–1 Antony makes it clear that he has deliberately worked the crowd in order to unleash their 'mischief'.

Imagine that, a day or so later, Antony reflects on his performance at Caesar's funeral. Write a dramatic monologue in which he runs through some of the highlights of his oration. Which strategies and ideas pleased him? Were there any surprises (either pleasant or unpleasant)? Did he feel that he accomplished all he set out to?

Wherein in what respect	**common pleasures** public
drachmaes silver coins	pleasure-grounds
walks parks	**brands** burning torches
arbours garden retreats	**forms** benches
orchards gardens	**windows** window shutters

ANTONY Yet hear me, countrymen, yet hear me speak.

ALL Peace ho, hear Antony, most noble Antony!

ANTONY Why, friends, you go to do you know not what.   225
        Wherein hath Caesar thus deserved your loves?
        Alas, you know not! I must tell you then:
        You have forgot the will I told you of.

ALL Most true. The will, let's stay and hear the will!

ANTONY Here is the will, and under Caesar's seal: 230
        To every Roman citizen he gives,
        To every several man, seventy-five drachmaes.

2 PLEBEIAN Most noble Caesar, we'll revenge his death!

3 PLEBEIAN O royal Caesar!

ANTONY Hear me with patience.   235

ALL Peace ho!

ANTONY Moreover, he hath left you all his walks,
        His private arbours and new-planted orchards,
        On this side Tiber; he hath left them you,
        And to your heirs for ever – common pleasures,   240
        To walk abroad and recreate yourselves.
        Here was a Caesar! When comes such another?

1 PLEBEIAN Never, never! Come, away, away!
        We'll burn his body in the holy place
        And with the brands fire the traitors' houses.   245
        Take up the body.

2 PLEBEIAN Go fetch fire!

3 PLEBEIAN Pluck down benches!

4 PLEBEIAN Pluck down forms, windows, anything!
                Exeunt Plebeians [with the body]

ANTONY Now let it work. Mischief, thou art afoot,   250
        Take thou what course thou wilt!

Enter SERVANT

                How now, fellow?

SERVANT Sir, Octavius is already come to Rome.

ANTONY Where is he?

SERVANT He and Lepidus are at Caesar's house.

ANTONY And thither will I straight to visit him.   255

Octavius' servant reports that Brutus and Cassius have fled Rome. Cinna the poet is interrogated by the Plebeians. Going where? Caesar's funeral. Friend or enemy? Friend.

---

1 Antony overheard (in groups of three to five)

Your production company, in a major television series, is to re-appraise Mark Antony's life and career some years after his death. In an interview Octavius' and Antony's servants tell you that they overheard everything Antony said just before they entered at Act 3 Scene 1, line 276, and Scene 2, line 251.

Write a script for the presenter to read after his interview with the servants. Your script should show how this revelation makes us re-examine everything Antony said or did after the assassination. It should also sum up this episode in Antony's life.

2 What happened to the conspirators? (in pairs)

Brutus and Cassius escape being killed by the mob only by riding 'like madmen through the gates of Rome' (Act 3 Scene 2, line 259). Improvise their conversation as they flee Rome, their dream of preserving the Roman Republic in tatters.

Other conspirators may not be so lucky. We hear no account of them, but surely not all of them could have escaped. Devise a fate which fits one of the other conspirators – Act 3 Scene 3 may give you ideas. You can act it out, or write it as a newspaper article or a short story.

3 Arguing with the director again! (in groups of four)

In Act 3 Scene 3 Cinna the poet (who had nothing at all to do with the conspiracy) is set upon by the enraged mob. This is another scene which the director wants to cut (see Act 2 Scenes 3 and 4). Again, the actors in this scene want to keep it. Both sides must have a good case. Argue for cutting or inclusion.

---

upon a wish exactly as I hoped	**things unluckily . . . fantasy** recent
Are rid have ridden	events weigh ominously on my mind
Belike presumably	**forth of doors** out of doors
they had . . . moved them they had	**directly** at once, to the point
news of how I had swayed the people	**bear me a bang** get a blow from me

He comes upon a wish. Fortune is merry,
And in this mood will give us anything.
SERVANT I heard him say Brutus and Cassius
Are rid like madmen through the gates of Rome.
ANTONY Belike they had some notice of the people,   260
How I had moved them. Bring me to Octavius.

Exeunt

Act 3 Scene 3
Rome A street

Enter CINNA THE POET, and after him the PLEBEIANS

CINNA THE POET I dreamt tonight that I did feast with Caesar,
And things unluckily charge my fantasy.
I have no will to wander forth of doors,
Yet something leads me forth.
1 PLEBEIAN What is your name?   5
2 PLEBEIAN Whither are you going?
3 PLEBEIAN Where do you dwell?
4 PLEBEIAN Are you a married man or a bachelor?
2 PLEBEIAN Answer every man directly.
1 PLEBEIAN Ay, and briefly.   10
4 PLEBEIAN Ay, and wisely.
3 PLEBEIAN Ay, and truly, you were best.
CINNA THE POET What is my name? Whither am I going? Where do I
dwell? Am I a married man or a bachelor? Then to answer every man
directly and briefly, wisely and truly. Wisely I say I am a bachelor.   15
2 PLEBEIAN That's as much as to say they are fools that marry. You'll
bear me a bang for that, I fear. Proceed directly.
CINNA THE POET Directly I am going to Caesar's funeral.
1 PLEBEIAN As a friend or an enemy?
CINNA THE POET As a friend.   20
2 PLEBEIAN That matter is answered directly.
4 PLEBEIAN For your dwelling – briefly.
CINNA THE POET Briefly, I dwell by the Capitol.
3 PLEBEIAN Your name, sir, truly.

Hearing his name, the common people accuse Cinna of conspiracy; he protests he's just a poet not a conspirator. They drag him off anyway, intending to burn the conspirators' houses.

1 The ordinary people remember (in groups of eight)

Before and during the Second World War, many Germans were incited by Hitler's oratory and became involved in acts of persecution which they later regretted.

Four of you are Plebeians 1–4 in old age, the other four a group of students who are taping senior citizens' reminiscences about events surrounding Caesar's assassination. The Plebeians describe the influence of Antony's oratory very fully, as well as how they now feel about their deeds that night. The students sharpen their memories with searching and detailed questions. Among other things, they want to know what happened to Cinna the poet – and why.

Royal Shakespeare Company, 1972. The death of Cinna the poet.

Pluck but   just tear   **turn him going**   finish him off

CINNA THE POET Truly, my name is Cinna.   25

1 PLEBEIAN Tear him to pieces, he's a conspirator.

CINNA THE POET I am Cinna the poet, I am Cinna the poet.

4 PLEBEIAN Tear him for his bad verses, tear him for his bad verses.

CINNA THE POET I am not Cinna the conspirator.

4 PLEBEIAN It is no matter, his name's Cinna. Pluck but his name out of   30
his heart and turn him going.

3 PLEBEIAN Tear him, tear him! Come, brands ho, firebrands! To
Brutus', to Cassius', burn all! Some to Decius' house, and some to
Casca's, some to Ligarius'! Away, go!

Exeunt all the Plebeians [forcing out Cinna]

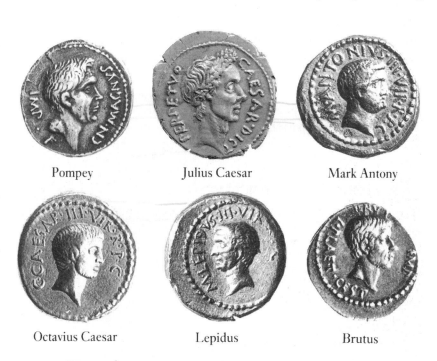

Pompey   Julius Caesar   Mark Antony

Octavius Caesar   Lepidus   Brutus

Looking back at Act 3
Activities for groups or individuals

1 Do you identify with a character?

All the major characters in the play have now spoken at some length. With which of the characters do you most identify? Write down some of the reasons why you feel in tune with that character.

With which character do you least identify – and why?

2 Newspaper billboards

Newspaper billboards give very brief summaries of the news. Write three of them, one for each scene. The billboards should catch the heart of the action.

3 Favourite lines

Act 3 contains some of Shakespeare's most memorable lines . . . and most eloquent persuasion. Select a handful of your own favourites and display them in a strikingly visual way. Compare your choices with others'.

4 The coffin and the cloak

Antony is a master at using visual objects to enhance his oratory. He makes striking references to Caesar's 'coffin' and to his 'mantle' (cloak). All producers have to decide how to display Caesar's corpse during the funeral speeches in order to make sense of Antony's words. Write some notes for the set designer and props manager about your own ideas. Study the photographs on pages 96 and 98 for help.

5 The crowd

Although only four Plebeians have lines in Act 3, many productions seek to give the Roman crowd a dynamic and energetic presence. Some do this by having the common people dotted amongst the actual audience. Some have used the audience as interactive participants in the funeral scene.

The picture on page 111 (top) shows the theatre audience mingling with cast members as Caesar's body lies alongside them.

- What do you think of this staging idea? Write a couple of paragraphs summarising its strengths and weaknesses.
- What other ideas do you have for exploiting the crowd scenes?

6 Assassination

The moment of Caesar's death. Compare this picture with the ones on page ix in the colour section and the front cover. Which do you find the most effective and why?

The Triumvirate organises a purge which includes family relatives. Antony shows contempt for Lepidus, and Octavius defends him.

1 What's the offence?

Reasons have to be given for a purge, even in a police state. Write, in precise legal language, the Triumvirate's charge against conspirators and their sympathisers.

2 A new view of Antony? (in groups of three)

Antony and his partners now control Rome. Take parts. Read lines 1–15 several times. Describe the kind of man Antony is now revealed to be.

What glimpses do you recall Shakespeare providing in Act 3 of the 'real' Antony that we see in this scene?

3 Gaining status (in groups of five or six)

You may have listened to or taken part in a conversation where what is said becomes unimportant because people only want to gain status and put each other down. They are trying to score points against each other.

Three of you read the parts of Antony, Octavius and Lepidus, the three members of the Triumvirate who each now rule one third of the Roman Empire – Europe, North Africa and Asia (comprising modern-day Turkey, Iran and Iraq). The others are a panel of judges who award points out of 10 when one triumvir 'scores' over another. Points can also be taken away for loss of status!

First, look over the whole scene individually and decide where points are scored and how many. Then play the whole scene, with the triumvirs breaking off to claim points. Everybody can argue about points, but the panel's decision is final.

Lastly, put the scene on tape. When you play it back, listen to see if the voices score the points they should.

---

cut off . . . legacies keep back some money from Caesar's will
slight, unmeritable insignificant, undeserving
threefold world three-part Roman Empire (see Activity 3 above)
voice side

proscription condemning to death, probably by adding legatees to the proscription list (see p. 173)
divers . . . loads blame for various things we have done
turn him off dismiss him
empty unburdened

Act 4 Scene 1
Rome

Enter ANTONY, OCTAVIUS, and LEPIDUS

ANTONY These many then shall die, their names are pricked.

OCTAVIUS Your brother too must die; consent you, Lepidus?

LEPIDUS I do consent.

OCTAVIUS   Prick him down, Antony.

LEPIDUS Upon condition Publius shall not live,
Who is your sister's son, Mark Antony.   5

ANTONY He shall not live – look, with a spot I damn him.
But, Lepidus, go you to Caesar's house,
Fetch the will hither, and we shall determine
How to cut off some charge in legacies.

LEPIDUS What, shall I find you here?   10

OCTAVIUS Or here or at the Capitol.

Exit Lepidus

ANTONY This is a slight, unmeritable man,
Meet to be sent on errands; is it fit,
The threefold world divided, he should stand
One of the three to share it?

OCTAVIUS   So you thought him   15
And took his voice who should be pricked to die
In our black sentence and proscription.

ANTONY Octavius, I have seen more days than you,
And though we lay these honours on this man
To ease ourselves of divers slanderous loads,   20
He shall but bear them as the ass bears gold,
To groan and sweat under the business,
Either led or driven, as we point the way;
And having brought our treasure where we will,
Then take we down his load and turn him off   25
(Like to the empty ass) to shake his ears
And graze in commons.

OCTAVIUS   You may do your will,
But he's a tried and valiant soldier.

Antony compares Lepidus to his horse. He and Octavius prepare for war against Brutus and Cassius. In the next scene Brutus asks Pindarus to bring his master Cassius to discuss Cassius' suspected misdeeds.

1 Lepidus, the third triumvir (in groups of three)

Lines 12–40 describe Lepidus, but Antony and Octavius clearly disagree about what he is like, which leaves the actor playing Lepidus free to decide on his character.

Rotating the parts, play Lepidus in lines 1–11 in as many ways as you can, experimenting with quite opposite interpretations. Have him say the thoughts in his head as he exits. Talk together about how the portrayal of Lepidus will influence an audience's view of Antony and Octavius.

2 Draw a cartoon picture of Lepidus

You are a staff officer in Mark Antony's army. You have in the past entertained your commander and the rest of his staff by drawing satirical cartoon portraits of other commanders and senior officers.

Study what Antony says about Lepidus, his fellow ruler of the Roman world, in lines 12–40. Now draw your cartoon portrait of the man Antony has described.

3 Recruiting in Asia (in two groups of up to five each)

When Brutus and Cassius return to the stage in Act 4 Scene 2, they have large armies raised in Asia (which, at that time, meant modern-day Turkey, Iraq and Iran).

Imagine one group of you are Republican recruiting officers who try to explain why Brutus and Cassius must defeat Antony and Octavius. The other group are Asians who challenge and ask questions. Assume that newspapers have kept the people of Turkey, Iraq and Iran well informed of recent events in Rome!

---

provender food
wind turn
corporal physical
in some taste to some extent
Which . . . his fashion (i.e. everything about him is second-hand and out of date)

property thing to be used (as in theatre 'prop')
covert hidden
at the stake in serious danger (image from bear-baiting)
bayed about with surrounded by (image from hunting)
ill incompetent, inadequate

ANTONY So is my horse, Octavius, and for that
I do appoint him store of provender. 30
It is a creature that I teach to fight,
To wind, to stop, to run directly on,
His corporal motion governed by my spirit.
And, in some taste, is Lepidus but so:
He must be taught and trained and bid go forth, 35
A barren-spirited fellow, one that feeds
On objects, arts, and imitations,
Which, out of use and staled by other men,
Begin his fashion. Do not talk of him
But as a property. And now, Octavius, 40
Listen great things. Brutus and Cassius
Are levying powers; we must straight make head.
Therefore let our alliance be combined,
Our best friends made, our means stretched,
And let us presently go sit in counsel, 45
How covert matters may be best disclosed
And open perils surest answerèd.
OCTAVIUS Let us do so, for we are at the stake
And bayed about with many enemies,
And some that smile have in their hearts, I fear, 50
Millions of mischiefs.

Exeunt

Act 4 Scene 2
Brutus' camp near Sardis in Asia

Drum. Enter BRUTUS, LUCILIUS, [Lucius,] and the army. Titinius
and PINDARUS meet them

BRUTUS Stand ho!
LUCILIUS Give the word ho, and stand!
BRUTUS What now, Lucilius, is Cassius near?
LUCILIUS He is at hand, and Pindarus is come
To do you salutation from his master. 5
BRUTUS He greets me well. Your master, Pindarus,
In his own change or by ill officers,
Hath given me some worthy cause to wish
Things done undone, but if he be at hand
I shall be satisfied.

Lucilius, returned from Cassius, reports that Cassius is no longer as friendly as before. Cassius enters with his army and says Brutus has wronged him. Brutus urges him to speak quietly.

---

1 'Enter Cassius and his powers' (in groups of about four)

Brutus' description of Cassius as 'A hot friend cooling' in line 19 makes it clear that there is friction between them. When Cassius enters with his military 'powers' at line 30 the tension is ratcheted up further.

As a group, work out how to stage the arrival of Cassius and his followers to create maximum impact. Where will you position or 'block' the characters? How does Brutus deploy his soldiers? How do the men speak to each other? Use the picture of the Globe stage on page 74 if you wish. Focus on blocking from the stage direction 'Low march within' after line 24 to line 42.

The stage directions call for two armies. Shakespeare's company was probably only about fifteen strong. If you have access to a hall or stage, join forces with one or more other groups in the class and try out your different blocking ideas for this opening confrontation. Explore ideas about sound effects and movement.

Decide which group's blocking combinations you like best and then rehearse and present your staging of the beginning of Brutus and Cassius' famous quarrel scene to the rest of the class.

---

instances signs (of friendship)
enforcèd strained, forced
hot at hand keen to be off at first
Low march within quiet marching
  drumbeat backstage
their crests the ridges of their necks
jades poor, inferior horses

Sink in the trial fail in the test
Sardis town in modern Turkey
horse in general entire cavalry
gently slowly
sober form serious manner
griefs complaints

PINDARUS   I do not doubt   10
          But that my noble master will appear
          Such as he is, full of regard and honour.
BRUTUS He is not doubted.
                    [*Brutus and Lucilius draw apart*]
                    A word, Lucilius,
          How he received you; let me be resolved.
LUCILIUS With courtesy and with respect enough,   15
          But not with such familiar instances,
          Nor with such free and friendly conference,
          As he hath used of old.
BRUTUS   Thou hast described
          A hot friend cooling. Ever note, Lucilius,
          When love begins to sicken and decay   20
          It useth an enforcèd ceremony.
          There are no tricks in plain and simple faith,
          But hollow men, like horses hot at hand,
          Make gallant show and promise of their mettle.
                    Low march within
          But when they should endure the bloody spur   25
          They fall their crests, and like deceitful jades
          Sink in the trial. Comes his army on?
LUCILIUS They mean this night in Sardis to be quartered.
          The greater part, the horse in general,
          Are come with Cassius.

                    Enter CASSIUS *and his powers*

BRUTUS   Hark, he is arrived.   30
          March gently on to meet him.
CASSIUS Stand ho!
BRUTUS Stand ho, speak the word along!
1 SOLDIER Stand!
2 SOLDIER Stand!   35
3 SOLDIER Stand!
CASSIUS Most noble brother, you have done me wrong.
BRUTUS Judge me, you gods! Wrong I mine enemies?
          And if not so, how should I wrong a brother?
CASSIUS Brutus, this sober form of yours hides wrongs,   40
          And when you do them –
BRUTUS   Cassius, be content,
          Speak your griefs softly, I do know you well.

Brutus and Cassius enter Brutus' tent for privacy. Inside, Brutus charges Cassius with greed and corruption. Cassius says that if such accusations came from anyone but Brutus, he would kill them.

1 Orchestrating the quarrel (in pairs)

Brutus and Cassius' quarrel holds the stage up to line 162 in a scene of strong emotion that must be carefully 'orchestrated' by the actors. Too loud and it will exhaust the audience, too restrained and it could bore them.

Imagine you have a volume control calibrated 1–10, where normal conversation registers 4. Talk together about the scene, suggesting volume levels at particular points. Remember that a big climax could be conveyed by silence, or intense emotion with a whisper.

Finally, read the scene aloud so that you think it sounds 'right', which does not necessarily mean as you planned it!

2 Canvas walls have ears (in groups of four)

Brutus and Cassius' quarrel could decide the fate of the Republican cause. It can only succeed if they are allies. As two of you read aloud lines 1–123, the other two imagine you are Lucilius and Titinius on guard, listening through the tent's thin walls. Though ordered not to interrupt, whisper to each other about:

- when you feel it must come to a duel
- how they manage to avoid a duel
- when you think either of them gains or loses honour.

Afterwards, one of you is Brutus, the other Cassius. Write a summary in modern English of your grievances against the other man. Then compare your lists. Who has the stronger case, do you think?

---

charges troops
noted publicly denounced
slighted off shamefully ignored
every nice offence . . . comment every trivial fault is criticised

condemned to have accused of having
itching palm greed for money
mart market, deal in
honours this corruption makes your financial corruption seem respectable

Before the eyes of both our armies here –
Which should perceive nothing but love from us –
Let us not wrangle. Bid them move away.   45
Then in my tent, Cassius, enlarge your griefs
And I will give you audience.

CASSIUS   Pindarus,
Bid our commanders lead their charges off
A little from this ground.

BRUTUS Lucius, do you the like, and let no man   50
Come to our tent till we have done our conference.
Let Lucilius and Titinius guard our door.

                    Exeunt [all but] Brutus and Cassius

Act 4 Scene 3
In Brutus' tent

CASSIUS That you have wronged me doth appear in this:
You have condemned and noted Lucius Pella
For taking bribes here of the Sardians,
Wherein my letters, praying on his side,
Because I knew the man, was slighted off.   5

BRUTUS You wronged yourself to write in such a case.

CASSIUS In such a time as this it is not meet
That every nice offence should bear his comment.

BRUTUS Let me tell you, Cassius, you yourself
Are much condemned to have an itching palm,   10
To sell and mart your offices for gold
To undeservers.

CASSIUS   I, an itching palm?
You know that you are Brutus that speaks this,
Or, by the gods, this speech were else your last.

BRUTUS The name of Cassius honours this corruption,   15
And chastisement doth therefore hide his head.

CASSIUS Chastisement?

BRUTUS Remember March, the Ides of March remember:
Did not great Julius bleed for justice' sake?

Caesar was killed to stamp out corruption, says Brutus. Cassius claims greater experience as a soldier. Brutus scorns Cassius' bad temper.

1 Management styles (in groups of four)

Plutarch records that 'when Caesar returned out of Africa and progressed up and down Italy, the things that pleased him best to see were the cities under Brutus' charge and government'.

You are a firm of management consultants who have been asked to write a report on the contrasting management styles of Cassius and Brutus.

- You can use the whole scene as evidence or just the opposite page.
- Talk together about how the two leaders deal with each other.
- How would they manage an army or city of many thousands?
- Interview another group who are posing as workers under the two leaders.

2 Quarrelling rhythms: the balance of power (in pairs or groups of three)

The rhythms of speech in this scene suggest the strength or weakness of the characters as much as what is said. They also suggest which character temporarily holds control over the dialogue at any one time.

Read carefully from 'I am a soldier, I' (line 30) to line 42. In this passage you will find many short and broken lines. Where the pauses fall will be crucial to the balance between Brutus and Cassius. Try reading it in different ways and decide which sounds right.

And not for justice if not for justice	**health** physical safety
sell the mighty space of our large	**choler** bad temper
honours profit by our high office	**testy humour** irritable, peevish nature
graspèd thus held in the hand like this	**spleen** malice, bad temper
bay bark at	**vaunting** boasting

What villain touched his body, that did stab   20
And not for justice? What, shall one of us,
That struck the foremost man of all this world,
But for supporting robbers, shall we now
Contaminate our fingers with base bribes
And sell the mighty space of our large honours   25
For so much trash as may be graspèd thus?
I had rather be a dog and bay the moon
Than such a Roman.

CASSIUS   Brutus, bait not me,
I'll not endure it. You forget yourself
To hedge me in. I am a soldier, I,   30
Older in practice, abler than yourself
To make conditions.

BRUTUS   Go to, you are not, Cassius!

CASSIUS I am.

BRUTUS I say you are not.

CASSIUS Urge me no more, I shall forget myself.   35
Have mind upon your health, tempt me no farther!

BRUTUS Away, slight man!

CASSIUS Is't possible?

BRUTUS   Hear me, for I will speak.
Must I give way and room to your rash choler?
Shall I be frighted when a madman stares?   40

CASSIUS O ye gods, ye gods, must I endure all this?

BRUTUS All this? Ay, more. Fret till your proud heart break.
Go show your slaves how choleric you are,
And make your bondmen tremble. Must I budge?
Must I observe you? Must I stand and crouch   45
Under your testy humour? By the gods,
You shall digest the venom of your spleen
Though it do split you. For, from this day forth,
I'll use you for my mirth, yea, for my laughter,
When you are waspish.

CASSIUS   Is it come to this?   50

BRUTUS You say you are a better soldier:
Let it appear so, make your vaunting true
And it shall please me well. For mine own part
I shall be glad to learn of noble men.

Brutus shrugs off Cassius' temper but is angry that Cassius refused him gold for his troops. Cassius says friends should not magnify each other's faults.

1 Money! Different attitudes (in pairs)

The quarrel between Brutus and Cassius in Act 4 Scene 3 is primarily over money to pay their troops. Look at what Brutus says about the matter in lines 69–82, and then at lines 100–5, where Cassius reveals something of his attitude to money.

Read the two speeches carefully several times, then talk together about how Shakespeare uses the issue of money to reveal the contrasting characters of Brutus and Cassius.

Now look back to Act 3 Scene 2, lines 120–50, and Act 4 Scene 1, lines 7–27, to see what is revealed of Antony's attitude to money. Write a short paragraph comparing Antony's views with those of Brutus and Cassius.

2 Design a coin (in groups of three or four)

Roman generals owned their armies and had to pay them out of their own pockets. Generals often minted their own coins with their own 'heads and tails' on them (see page 109). Like today's coins, they carried designs which symbolised something

important to those who minted them. This Italian coin of 90 BC shows the Italian lion goring the Roman wolf at a time when Rome was at war with the other states and tribes of Italy.

As a design consultancy, come up with a series of designs for coin 'tails' for Brutus or Cassius. Your designs should make the soldiers think about what they are fighting for when they get paid.

Write a short explanation beside each design, which can of course be much larger than the actual coins would be.

---

durst not   dared not
moved me   irritated me
tempted him   provoked him

honesty   uprightness, integrity
indirection   dishonesty
rascal counters   rubbishy coins

CASSIUS   You wrong me every way, you wrong me, Brutus.   55
           I said an elder soldier, not a better.
           Did I say 'better'?
BRUTUS   If you did, I care not.
CASSIUS   When Caesar lived, he durst not thus have moved me.
BRUTUS   Peace, peace, you durst not so have tempted him.
CASSIUS   I durst not?   60
BRUTUS   No.
CASSIUS   What? Durst not tempt him?
BRUTUS   For your life you durst not.
CASSIUS   Do not presume too much upon my love,
           I may do that I shall be sorry for.
BRUTUS   You have done that you should be sorry for.   65
           There is no terror, Cassius, in your threats,
           For I am armed so strong in honesty
           That they pass by me as the idle wind,
           Which I respect not. I did send to you
           For certain sums of gold, which you denied me,   70
           For I can raise no money by vile means.
           By heaven, I had rather coin my heart
           And drop my blood for drachmaes than to wring
           From the hard hands of peasants their vile trash
           By any indirection. I did send   75
           To you for gold to pay my legions,
           Which you denied me. Was that done like Cassius?
           Should I have answered Caius Cassius so?
           When Marcus Brutus grows so covetous
           To lock such rascal counters from his friends,   80
           Be ready, gods, with all your thunderbolts,
           Dash him to pieces!
CASSIUS   I denied you not.
BRUTUS   You did.
CASSIUS   I did not. He was but a fool that brought
           My answer back. Brutus hath rived my heart.   85
           A friend should bear his friend's infirmities,
           But Brutus makes mine greater than they are.
BRUTUS   I do not, till you practise them on me.

Stung by Brutus' criticism, Cassius asks Brutus to kill him. Brutus relents, admits blame himself and resolves to ignore Cassius' temper in future.

1 A notable friendship (in groups of three or four)

After Cassius' outburst at lines 93–107, Brutus and Cassius suddenly become firm friends, and so they remain. The cultivation of friendship was an all-important duty in the ancient world. In the year of Caesar's death, Cicero wrote as follows in his essay *Of Friendship*:

> Take away the bond of kindly feeling from the world, and no house or city can stand. Even the fields will no longer be cultivated. If that sounds exaggerated, consider the opposite state of affairs: note the disasters that come from dissension and enmity. When there is internal hatred and division, no home or country in the world is strong enough to avoid destruction.

At the end of this scene, Brutus is reading a book. Imagine he was reading the passage from Cicero above. He is full of sadness as Cicero has just been killed in the purge instigated by Antony, Octavius and Lepidus. Suppose it spurs Brutus on to confide his thoughts in a soliloquy at line 274, which you can write.

As you read through, gather material from the rest of the scene for your soliloquy. In public, Brutus shows true Stoic self-control as he and the generals mull over news from Rome, but alone he can ponder aloud the whole enterprise he undertook with Cassius.

Research together, but write individually. Concentrate your ideas into poetry, but not necessarily Shakespearean verse. Dramatic poetry should be condensed and fast moving – forty lines maximum.

Checked rebuked, told off
conned by rote learned by heart
Pluto's mine infinite wealth (Pluto, Roman god of the Underworld, was said to possess all mineral wealth)
If that thou beest if you are

dishonour ... humour your bad behaviour will be tolerated
much enforcèd when struck violently
blood ill-tempered an unbalanced disposition

CASSIUS You love me not.

BRUTUS   I do not like your faults.

CASSIUS A friendly eye could never see such faults.   90

BRUTUS A flatterer's would not, though they do appear
    As huge as high Olympus.

CASSIUS Come, Antony, and young Octavius, come,
    Revenge yourselves alone on Cassius,
    For Cassius is a-weary of the world: 95
    Hated by one he loves, braved by his brother,
    Checked like a bondman, all his faults observed,
    Set in a notebook, learned, and conned by rote,
    To cast into my teeth. O, I could weep
    My spirit from mine eyes! There is my dagger   100
    And here my naked breast: within, a heart
    Dearer than Pluto's mine, richer than gold.
    If that thou beest a Roman take it forth,
    I that denied thee gold will give my heart:
    Strike as thou didst at Caesar. For I know   105
    When thou didst hate him worst thou loved'st him better
    Than ever thou loved'st Cassius.

BRUTUS   Sheathe your dagger.
    Be angry when you will, it shall have scope;
    Do what you will, dishonour shall be humour.
    O Cassius, you are yokèd with a lamb   110
    That carries anger as the flint bears fire,
    Who, much enforcèd, shows a hasty spark
    And straight is cold again.

CASSIUS   Hath Cassius lived
    To be but mirth and laughter to his Brutus
    When grief and blood ill-tempered vexeth him?   115

BRUTUS When I spoke that, I was ill-tempered too.

CASSIUS Do you confess so much? Give me your hand.

BRUTUS And my heart too.

CASSIUS   O Brutus!

BRUTUS   What's the matter?

CASSIUS Have not you love enough to bear with me
    When that rash humour which my mother gave me   120
    Makes me forgetful?

BRUTUS   Yes, Cassius, and from henceforth
    When you are over-earnest with your Brutus,
    He'll think your mother chides, and leave you so.

A poet tries to intercede and reconcile Brutus and Cassius. With uncharacteristic fury, Brutus throws him out. Cassius is surprised. Brutus explains that his wife is dead.

1 Should the Poet be cut? (in groups of six to eight)

The brief episode where a Poet interrupts Brutus and Cassius' conversation (lines 124–38) follows pretty closely the Greek historian Plutarch's account of events. But Shakespeare could easily have left him out. Talk together about a) why the Poet *was* included and b) whether the play is better with his brief part cut completely.

2 Portia's final moments

a **Show her death** (in pairs). The audience does not see Portia's death; Brutus reports it. One of you is Brutus, the other Portia. Brutus reads aloud lines 152–6; Portia silently enacts the events described, ending at a freeze-frame or tableau that captures the moment of her death.

b **Portia's suicide note** (in groups of three). Plutarch records how Portia put burning coal in her mouth and choked to death. Talk together about what could have forced Portia to commit suicide and why she decided to do it this way.
 – Write her suicide note.
 – Exchange your note with another group and discuss the differences.

c **A covering letter**. Someone must have sent Portia's suicide note to Brutus. Decide who it might have been and write the letter they would have sent to Brutus with Portia's note.

d **Why does Portia die offstage?** (in small groups) Talk together about the reasons Shakespeare might have had for not showing Portia's death as part of the main action of the play.

---

vildly vilely, wretchedly
cynic follower of Cynic philosophy (see p. 172)
when . . . his time when he can choose the right time to show it
jigging rhyming

your philosophy (Brutus was a Stoic – see p. 173)
give place give way
accidental evils chance bad luck
distract mad

Enter a POET, [LUCILIUS *and Titinius*]

POET Let me go in to see the generals.
    There is some grudge between 'em, 'tis not meet   125
    They be alone.
LUCILIUS You shall not come to them.
POET Nothing but death shall stay me.
CASSIUS How now, what's the matter?
POET For shame, you generals, what do you mean?   130
    Love and be friends, as two such men should be,
    For I have seen more years, I'm sure, than ye.
CASSIUS Ha, ha, how vildly doth this cynic rhyme!
BRUTUS Get you hence, sirrah; saucy fellow, hence!
CASSIUS Bear with him, Brutus, 'tis his fashion.   135
BRUTUS I'll know his humour when he knows his time.
    What should the wars do with these jigging fools?
    Companion, hence!
CASSIUS   Away, away, be gone!

                                       Exit Poet

BRUTUS Lucilius and Titinius, bid the commanders
    Prepare to lodge their companies tonight.   140
CASSIUS And come yourselves, and bring Messala with you
    Immediately to us.

                     [Exeunt Lucilius and Titinius]

BRUTUS *[To Lucius within]* Lucius, a bowl of wine!
CASSIUS I did not think you could have been so angry.
BRUTUS O Cassius, I am sick of many griefs.
CASSIUS Of your philosophy you make no use   145
    If you give place to accidental evils.
BRUTUS No man bears sorrow better. Portia is dead.
CASSIUS Ha? Portia?
BRUTUS She is dead.
CASSIUS How scaped I killing when I crossed you so?   150
    O insupportable and touching loss!
    Upon what sickness?
BRUTUS   Impatient of my absence,
    And grief that young Octavius with Mark Antony
    Have made themselves so strong – for with her death
    That tidings came. With this she fell distract   155
    And, her attendants absent, swallowed fire.

Reconciled, Brutus and Cassius drink wine. Titinius and Messala enter to report that the Triumvirate has executed Cicero and a hundred other senators, and now approach Philippi.

---

1 Wine and tapers (in groups of three)

Colonising Romans 'civilised' their conquered subjects by encouraging them to cultivate vineyards. Wine growing was an art of peace and wine still has symbolic or religious meanings. Many customs and rituals use wine or alcohol.

In the gathering darkness suggested by Lucius' tapers, Brutus and Cassius drain their bowl of wine. As he would at home, Lucius brings hospitality to Cassius even though they are in a tent 850 miles from Rome and Portia is dead.

Read and mime the actions from Lucius' entrance to his exit (lines 158–62). These five lines might take quite a long time to act out on stage. Feel your way into the characters' minds as you act. Compare their thoughts when you have finished.

This moment echoes Act 2 Scene 2, where Brutus and Caesar drank together on the morning of Caesar's assassination. In role as Brutus or Cassius, write a short monologue on how your relationship with your co-conspirator has evolved. Compare your responses with those of other group members.

2 The bringer of bad news (in groups of four)

No subject ever wants to be the bringer of bad news to a ruler, yet a wise ruler values those who are frank.

Hold a conversation between Messala and Titinius about how to break the news of Portia's death to Brutus, then act out lines 181–97, and finally talk together about Brutus' reaction, after you have left the tent (after line 238).

---

call in . . . necessities consider what we must do
Bending their expedition moving rapidly

Philippi (pronounced fye-lip-eye) where the Republicans were finally defeated in 42 BC
selfsame tenor very similar news

CASSIUS And died so?

BRUTUS   Even so.

CASSIUS   O ye immortal gods!

Enter BOY [LUCIUS] *with wine and tapers*

BRUTUS Speak no more of her. Give me a bowl of wine.
         In this I bury all unkindness, Cassius. *Drinks*

CASSIUS My heart is thirsty for that noble pledge.   160
         Fill, Lucius, till the wine o'erswell the cup,
         I cannot drink too much of Brutus' love. [*Drinks*]
                                    [*Exit Lucius*]

Enter TITINIUS *and* MESSALA

BRUTUS Come in, Titinius; welcome, good Messala.
         Now sit we close about this taper here
         And call in question our necessities.   165

CASSIUS Portia, art thou gone?

BRUTUS   No more, I pray you.
         Messala, I have here receivèd letters
         That young Octavius and Mark Antony
         Come down upon us with a mighty power,
         Bending their expedition toward Philippi.   170

MESSALA Myself have letters of the selfsame tenor.

BRUTUS With what addition?

MESSALA That by proscription and bills of outlawry
         Octavius, Antony, and Lepidus
         Have put to death an hundred senators.   175

BRUTUS Therein our letters do not well agree:
         Mine speak of seventy senators that died
         By their proscriptions, Cicero being one.

CASSIUS Cicero one?

MESSALA   Cicero is dead,
         And by that order of proscription.   180
         Had you your letters from your wife, my lord?

BRUTUS No, Messala.

MESSALA Nor nothing in your letters writ of her?

BRUTUS Nothing, Messala.

MESSALA   That, methinks, is strange.

Brutus philosophically receives news of Portia's death, then turns to military tactics. Take battle to the enemy, he says. Let battle come to us, says Cassius. Brutus insists his plan is best.

---

1 The Free Rome Broadcasting Network (in groups of up to six)

Republicans at home and in exile keep in close touch. Those at home keep the Republican flame burning among the people; those abroad raise armies to recapture Rome. Imagine there is a broadcasting network to keep all Republicans informed.

Put together a radio or TV programme to emphasise the horrors of Triumvirate rule, yet celebrate Republican achievement and give heart to those who carry on the struggle. Use excerpts from the play as tape recordings or newsreel, and invent interviews with leading Republicans.

2 Good friends – good generals? (in groups of three)

Titinius and Lucilius have witnessed Brutus and Cassius' quarrel. But when Titinius and Messala enter (after line 162) Brutus and Cassius are drinking companionably together. Bring all three officers together to talk over the change in their two leaders and guess at reasons for it. Then also wonder if the right military tactic has been chosen for tomorrow's battle. Set your conversation in the officers' mess the following morning.

3 'a tide in the affairs of men' (in groups of three or four)

In the days of sail, trading ships often had to wait for the right wind and tide. Too long a wait and the cargo might lose its value, especially if it were perishable. Sail at the wrong time and the ship could be wrecked. Either way investors would lose money. Talk together about whether what Brutus says in lines 218–24 is true of life as you know it. Devise and present a short improvisation that shows him to be right or wrong.

I have . . . in art as you   I am as learned [in Stoicism] as you
presently   immediately
offence   damage, harm
of force   of necessity
Do stand . . . forced affection   show only a grudging loyalty

new added   newly reinforced
tried the utmost of   made the greatest demands on
Omitted   (i.e. if they fail to take the opportunity)
bound in   limited, confined to

BRUTUS Why ask you? Hear you aught of her in yours?   185
MESSALA No, my lord.
BRUTUS Now as you are a Roman tell me true.
MESSALA Then like a Roman bear the truth I tell,
    For certain she is dead, and by strange manner.
BRUTUS Why, farewell, Portia. We must die, Messala.   190
    With meditating that she must die once,
    I have the patience to endure it now.
MESSALA Even so, great men great losses should endure.
CASSIUS I have as much of this in art as you,
    But yet my nature could not bear it so.   195
BRUTUS Well, to our work alive. What do you think
    Of marching to Philippi presently?
CASSIUS I do not think it good.
BRUTUS   Your reason?
CASSIUS   This it is:
    'Tis better that the enemy seek us,
    So shall he waste his means, weary his soldiers,   200
    Doing himself offence, whilst we, lying still,
    Are full of rest, defence, and nimbleness.
BRUTUS Good reasons must of force give place to better:
    The people 'twixt Philippi and this ground
    Do stand but in a forced affection,   205
    For they have grudged us contribution.
    The enemy, marching along by them,
    By them shall make a fuller number up,
    Come on refreshed, new added, and encouraged,
    From which advantage shall we cut him off   210
    If at Philippi we do face him there,
    These people at our back.
CASSIUS   Hear me, good brother.
BRUTUS Under your pardon. You must note beside
    That we have tried the utmost of our friends,
    Our legions are brimful, our cause is ripe;   215
    The enemy increaseth every day,
    We, at the height, are ready to decline.
    There is a tide in the affairs of men
    Which, taken at the flood, leads on to fortune;
    Omitted, all the voyage of their life   220
    Is bound in shallows and in miseries.

Cassius agrees to march to face the enemy at Philippi. After a harmonious leave-taking, Brutus is left to sleep. He asks Lucius for music.

---

1 The last night of the Roman Republic

'The deep of night is crept upon our talk', says Brutus. Capture the mood of the scene in your own poem about what happens between the entry of Lucius (line 158) and the departure of the generals (line 238). You may start or end each verse with this chorus, change the chorus if you wish, or cut it altogether:

> The last night of the Roman Republic
> Five centuries old
> Tapers flickered in Brutus' tent
> And darkness fell and fell.

Think your way into Brutus' hopes, fears, memories, sadness, bravery, friendship . . . everything that goes on under the calm surface.

2 Calm after the storm (in groups of four)

A significant number of lines 30–42 of this scene (p. 121) were short and broken. Here, lines 229–40 are much more regular, though nearly all shared. Read both sets of lines with careful regard for the rhythm. Talk together about the contrasting effects.

3 Strictly for the record (in two pairs)

Two persons as Lucilius and Messala think of questions to ask the two leaders about their reconciliation. The other pair, as Brutus and Cassius, re-read the scene, as if going over it in memory to prepare for their interviews. Then go ahead and ask the questions.

---

ventures investments, goods risked in trade
with your will go on as you wish, we shall advance
nature . . . necessity our bodies need caring for
niggard put off temporarily

hence go from this place
gown dressing gown (see also p. 60)
instrument musical instrument (probably a lute)
Poor knave poor lad
o'erwatched weary from lack of sleep

On such a full sea are we now afloat,
And we must take the current when it serves
Or lose our ventures.

CASSIUS   Then with your will go on,
We'll along ourselves and meet them at Philippi.   225

BRUTUS The deep of night is crept upon our talk,
And nature must obey necessity,
Which we will niggard with a little rest.
There is no more to say?

CASSIUS   No more. Good night.
Early tomorrow will we rise and hence.   230

BRUTUS Lucius!

Enter LUCIUS

My gown.

                                        [*Exit Lucius*]
Farewell, good Messala.
Good night, Titinius. Noble, noble Cassius,
Good night and good repose.

CASSIUS   O my dear brother!
This was an ill beginning of the night.
Never come such division 'tween our souls!   235
Let it not, Brutus.

Enter LUCIUS *with the gown*

BRUTUS   Everything is well.

CASSIUS Good night, my lord.

BRUTUS   Good night, good brother.

TITINIUS AND MESSALA Good night, Lord Brutus.

BRUTUS   Farewell every one.
                    Exeunt [*Cassius, Titinius, Messala*]
Give me the gown. Where is thy instrument?

LUCIUS Here in the tent.

BRUTUS   What, thou speak'st drowsily.   240
Poor knave, I blame thee not, thou art o'erwatched.
Call Claudio and some other of my men,
I'll have them sleep on cushions in my tent.

LUCIUS Varrus and Claudio!

Varrus and Claudio are summoned to sleep in Brutus' tent. Lucius plays music but falls asleep. While Brutus reads, the ghost of Caesar enters.

1 History above and below stairs (groups of five to eight)

Servants often provide biographical detail about the private lives of historical figures. In Act 4 Shakespeare shows how all the leaders – Antony, Octavius, Brutus and Cassius – behave in private.

Imagine that the historian Plutarch and his researchers have found the personal attendants of the four leaders in old age and are about to interview them.

Divide into 'historians' and 'servants'. While the servants refresh their memories about their masters (and perhaps read on in the play, as Cassius' servant Pindarus should) the historians prepare questions to ask. These might include: How did he treat his wife? How would he deal with a slave's petty theft? What kind of vehicle did he own? Build a picture of the leaders from both the play and your own imaginations.

2 Compose Lucius' song (in pairs)

No words or music survive for Lucius' song, and as musical directors you have to supply them. Think about the mood needed and the right words to express it. Compose your own music or set your words to a tune you know already. You can adapt well-known tunes by speeding them up or slowing them down.

3 Brutus: what's your reaction? (in pairs)

Brutus has dealt stoically with Portia's death and is reconciled to Cassius. Now Shakespeare shows him treating his servant Lucius considerately and generously. Look back at this scene, then write a short paragraph outlining your response to the Brutus you see here.

4 A notable friendship

Now you have reached this point in your reading, you will be able to complete the activity described on page 124.

raise rouse	**young bloods** hot-blooded
otherwise bethink me change my mind	youngsters
	murd'rous death-like
strain tune, song	**leaden mace** heavy staff
an't if it	**ill** badly, poorly

Enter VARRUS *and* CLAUDIO

VARRUS Calls my lord? 245

BRUTUS I pray you, sirs, lie in my tent and sleep,
     It may be I shall raise you by and by
     On business to my brother Cassius.

VARRUS So please you, we will stand and watch your pleasure.

BRUTUS I will not have it so. Lie down, good sirs, 250
     It may be I shall otherwise bethink me.
              [Varrus and Claudio lie down]
     Look, Lucius, here's the book I sought for so,
     I put it in the pocket of my gown.

LUCIUS I was sure your lordship did not give it me.

BRUTUS Bear with me, good boy, I am much forgetful. 255
     Canst thou hold up thy heavy eyes awhile
     And touch thy instrument a strain or two?

LUCIUS Ay, my lord, an't please you.

BRUTUS   It does, my boy.
     I trouble thee too much, but thou art willing.

LUCIUS It is my duty, sir. 260

BRUTUS I should not urge thy duty past thy might,
     I know young bloods look for a time of rest.

LUCIUS I have slept, my lord, already.

BRUTUS It was well done and thou shalt sleep again,
     I will not hold thee long. If I do live 265
     I will be good to thee.
              Music, and a song
     This is a sleepy tune. O murd'rous slumber,
     Layest thou thy leaden mace upon my boy,
     That plays thee music? Gentle knave, good night,
     I will not do thee so much wrong to wake thee. 270
     If thou dost nod thou break'st thy instrument.
     I'll take it from thee and, good boy, good night.
     Let me see, let me see, is not the leaf turned down
     Where I left reading? Here it is, I think.

Enter the GHOST OF CAESAR

     How ill this taper burns! Ha, who comes here? 275

Promising a second appearance, the ghost disappears. Brutus wakes the servants and orders immediate preparations for marching to Philippi to do battle with Antony and Octavius.

1 Caesar's ghost

Ghosts were highly significant for Elizabethans. They believed that ghosts could be good or bad, silent or talkative, truthful or deceptive. Evil spirits could disguise themselves to mislead mortals. If you knew how to talk to a ghost, you could gain valuable (or misleading) information about the past, present or future.

a **The first appearance of Caesar's ghost** (in pairs). Read or stage lines 273–88 as dramatically as you can.

b **The ghost's second appearance** (in groups of six). In Act 5 Scene 5, lines 17–19, we learn that Brutus did see the ghost again, the night before the crucial battle of Philippi, but the play does not give us that scene. Improvise the ghost's second appearance. Work in two groups: one group as Brutus and one as the ghost.

  – **Brutus' group**. Think about how the ghost should be spoken to. Prepare questions for Brutus to ask.
  – **Ghost group**. Decide who the ghost is and what his motives are. Anticipate Brutus' questions, and decide what information to give him, and how to speak, straight or riddling.

  Now play out the second appearance.

c **What should Caesar's ghost look like?** (in groups of four) Every director must decide how to portray the 'monstrous apparition': Bloodstains? Larger than life? A floating head? Voiceover rather than physical presence? Talk together about how you could present Caesar's ghost to make the greatest impression on the audience.

d **'Art thou some god, some angel, or some devil?'** Write six more lines to add to the end of Brutus' speech (lines 275–81), beginning 'If you are a god'.

upon me towards me	**set on his powers** get his forces
stare stand on end	moving
false out of tune	**betimes** early in the morning

I think it is the weakness of mine eyes
That shapes this monstrous apparition.
It comes upon me. Art thou any thing?
Art thou some god, some angel, or some devil,
That mak'st my blood cold and my hair to stare?   280
Speak to me what thou art.
GHOST Thy evil spirit, Brutus.
BRUTUS   Why com'st thou?
GHOST To tell thee thou shalt see me at Philippi.
BRUTUS Well, then I shall see thee again?
GHOST Ay, at Philippi.   285
BRUTUS Why, I will see thee at Philippi then.

                                        [*Exit Ghost*]

Now I have taken heart thou vanishest.
Ill spirit, I would hold more talk with thee.
Boy, Lucius! Varrus! Claudio! Sirs, awake!
Claudio!   290
LUCIUS The strings, my lord, are false.
BRUTUS He thinks he still is at his instrument.
Lucius, awake!
LUCIUS My lord?
BRUTUS Didst thou dream, Lucius, that thou so cried'st out? 295
LUCIUS My lord, I do not know that I did cry.
BRUTUS Yes, that thou didst. Didst thou see anything?
LUCIUS Nothing, my lord.
BRUTUS Sleep again, Lucius. Sirrah Claudio!
[*To Varrus*] Fellow, thou, awake!   300
VARRUS My lord?
CLAUDIO My lord?
BRUTUS Why did you so cry out, sirs, in your sleep?
BOTH Did we, my lord?
BRUTUS   Ay. Saw you anything?
VARRUS No, my lord, I saw nothing.
CLAUDIO   Nor I, my lord.   305
BRUTUS Go and commend me to my brother Cassius.
Bid him set on his powers betimes before,
And we will follow.
BOTH   It shall be done, my lord.

                                        Exeunt

Looking back at Act 4
Activities for groups or individuals

1 From Rome to Asia

The action of the play switches at the beginning of Act 4 Scene 2 from Rome to Asia. Work out a set design for one of the three scenes in the act. Add notes to explain how you would manage the scene-shifting so that the attention of the audience is not lost.

2 Is updating possible?

Some productions of *Julius Caesar* are given a setting in modern times, for example fascist Italy of the 1930s. Imagine that you have been invited to direct a production set in the twenty-first century. Take one of the scenes in Act 4, and talk together about a possible modern setting and about appropriate costumes for characters.

3 Giving Octavius a presence

Octavius does not appear in the play until Act 4, yet by that time he is already established as a key member of the Triumvirate. How would you organise the opening of Act 4 to give him a genuine stage presence and authority?

4 Keeping up the tempo

Many critics feel that the last two acts of the play are an anti-climax after the superlative assassination and funeral scenes in Act 3. Quickly remind yourself of the events of Act 4, then write notes for your cast about how to sustain the dramatic energy through this act.

5 Brutus and Cassius

Study the picture below in which Cassius (left) and Brutus argue passionately.

- How effectively does this picture capture the moment when two friends fall out?
- Which line(s) in Act 4 Scene 3 are being spoken here? Give your reasons.
- In this production Brutus and Cassius wore modern business suits in the first three acts. They now dress in combat fatigues. What do you think the director had in mind?

Octavius and Antony argue about why the enemy has come down to them, and both vie for leadership in the coming battle. Brutus and Cassius enter with their army.

---

1 Leaders disagree – again (in pairs)

The first time we saw Antony and Octavius together they argued. Here, the two men disagree over the advance of the Republican army and over which of them should lead the Triumvirate forces. Read lines 1–20, missing out the Messenger's speech. Describe the two leaders' different styles of arguing.

Antony and Octavius' confrontation mirrors that between Brutus and Cassius in the previous scene. Look back at Act 4 Scene 3, then make a list of how similar are a) the issues at the centre of the arguments and b) the ways in which the four men quarrel.

2 Right of the line (in two groups of four each)

According to Plutarch, the battlefield of Philippi looked like this:

Antony (right)		Octavius (left)
v		v
Cassius (left)		Brutus (right)

The superior general always fought on the right of the line of battle: that's why lines 16–20 are so important. Shakespeare retains who fought whom, but leaves right and left open to directors of the play to decide. One of your groups consists of the Triumvirate leaders and the other the Republican leaders, with two military experts to arbitrate on each side. Hold frank discussions between the leaders about who should fight on the right. Take into account military advantage, personal status and integrity, age and experience.

---

battles armies
warn us challenge us
I am in their bosoms I know what they are thinking
could be . . . other places would rather be somewhere else
face pretence (of bravery)

bloody sign red flag (the Roman battle signal)
lead your battle softly on advance your army slowly
cross me oppose me
exigent crisis
parley talks under truce

Act 5 Scene 1
The battlefield at Philippi in Greece

Enter OCTAVIUS, ANTONY, *and their army*

OCTAVIUS Now, Antony, our hopes are answerèd.
    You said the enemy would not come down
    But keep the hills and upper regions.
    It proves not so: their battles are at hand,
    They mean to warn us at Philippi here,   5
    Answering before we do demand of them.
ANTONY Tut, I am in their bosoms, and I know
    Wherefore they do it. They could be content
    To visit other places and come down
    With fearful bravery, thinking by this face   10
    To fasten in our thoughts that they have courage.
    But 'tis not so.

Enter a MESSENGER

MESSENGER   Prepare you, generals,
    The enemy comes on in gallant show,
    Their bloody sign of battle is hung out,
    And something to be done immediately.   15
ANTONY Octavius, lead your battle softly on
    Upon the left hand of the even field.
OCTAVIUS Upon the right hand I, keep thou the left.
ANTONY Why do you cross me in this exigent?
OCTAVIUS I do not cross you, but I will do so.   20
March

Drum. Enter BRUTUS, CASSIUS, *and their army;* [LUCILIUS,
Titinius, MESSALA, *and others*]

BRUTUS They stand and would have parley.
CASSIUS Stand fast, Titinius, we must out and talk.

The generals parley, trading taunts and accusations. Octavius vows vengeance for Julius Caesar's death.

1 Trading insults (in groups of four)

Before battle commences the four generals meet to parley, but quickly start taunting each other. Brutus' opening salvo 'Words before blows' underlines a major issue: the importance of language to the action of the play. Antony for example is keen to stress the physical, bodily consequences of the conspirators' words: 'the hole you made in Caesar's heart'.

Take parts and read lines 27–66. As you do so, concentrate on the following:

- Begin line 27 at a whisper. With each subsequent speech, increase the volume slightly until you are virtually shouting the lines.
- Discuss how you could arrange ('block') the four characters on stage to create maximum impact when they hurl insults at each other. For example, some productions have the men on opposite sides of a table (which might then be overturned, along with other furniture).
- In lines 39–44 Antony strikingly creates four powerful, insulting similes to hurl at his enemies. Two of you are Antony. Deliver the lines simultaneously (or with a slight time delay or echo effect) as you circle round the seated Brutus and Cassius. How menacing can you make them? Afterwards talk about how the experience felt.
- Brutus is silent for some time after Antony's speech (lines 39–44). What is he thinking? Which of Antony's words have really grated on him? Write down his thoughts.

2 Is battle inevitable? (in groups of four)

Can battle be avoided? Talk together about whether honourable negotiation might be possible and desirable after line 58.

---

answer on their charge wait until they attack
Make forth go forward
posture nature
Hybla Sicilian town famous for its honey

might have ruled could have had his way
cause business at hand
proof testing
goes up is sheathed
Have added slaughter to has also been killed by

OCTAVIUS Mark Antony, shall we give sign of battle?

ANTONY No, Caesar, we will answer on their charge.

Make forth, the generals would have some words.   25

OCTAVIUS Stir not until the signal.

BRUTUS Words before blows; is it so, countrymen?

OCTAVIUS Not that we love words better, as you do.

BRUTUS Good words are better than bad strokes, Octavius.

ANTONY In your bad strokes, Brutus, you give good words.   30

Witness the hole you made in Caesar's heart,

Crying, 'Long live, hail, Caesar!'

CASSIUS   Antony,

The posture of your blows are yet unknown;

But for your words, they rob the Hybla bees

And leave them honeyless.

ANTONY   Not stingless too?   35

BRUTUS O yes, and soundless too,

For you have stolen their buzzing, Antony,

And very wisely threat before you sting.

ANTONY Villains! You did not so when your vile daggers

Hacked one another in the sides of Caesar.   40

You showed your teeth like apes and fawned like hounds,

And bowed like bondmen, kissing Caesar's feet,

Whilst damnèd Casca, like a cur, behind

Struck Caesar on the neck. O you flatterers!

CASSIUS Flatterers? Now, Brutus, thank yourself.   45

This tongue had not offended so today

If Cassius might have ruled.

OCTAVIUS Come, come, the cause. If arguing make us sweat,

The proof of it will turn to redder drops.

Look,   50

I draw a sword against conspirators;

When think you that the sword goes up again?

Never, till Caesar's three and thirty wounds

Be well avenged, or till another Caesar

Have added slaughter to the sword of traitors.   55

BRUTUS Caesar, thou canst not die by traitors' hands

Unless thou bring'st them with thee.

OCTAVIUS   So I hope.

I was not born to die on Brutus' sword.

Cassius insults the triumvirs. Octavius defies him and the triumvirs leave with their troops. Cassius, whose birthday it is, confides to Messala his newfound respect for omens.

---

1 Octavius – what's he like? (in small groups)

Octavius does not appear in the play until Act 4, but he makes quite an impression. Look back at what he says in this scene (and how he says it), then combine your group's ideas into a short written paragraph about his character. How closely does your assessment match the impression created by the actor playing Octavius in the photograph on page 165?

2 Cassius – 'all is on the hazard' (in small groups)

Read together lines 70–91, changing speakers at each full stop. Cassius seems to have become particularly superstitious. Unlike the super-confident Octavius ('If you dare fight today'), he speaks of fateful storms and chance throws of the dice ('on the hazard'). Furthermore, it's Cassius' birthday and he is conscious of powerful natural omens such as the carrion birds ('ravens, crows, and kites') that shadow his army.

One of you now becomes Cassius. The rest put him in the 'hot seat'. What has brought about the change in his philosophy and beliefs? How will it affect his approach to the crucial battle at Philippi? Quiz him about the assassination of Caesar and where and why it all went wrong.

3 Waiting to do battle

Before a big battle, soldiers often write down their thoughts in letters or diaries. After Cassius' speech (lines 70–88), and the parley and conversation of the night before, Messala has an in-depth knowledge of Cassius' state of mind. Writing as Messala, see if you can pin down your leader's state of mind on paper. Speculate whether it has been sensed by the troops or has affected their morale.

---

strain family
masker amateur actor and dancer
reveller lover of parties
stomachs courage, inclination
bark ship, vessel
on the hazard to be played for

Epicurus Greek philosopher (see p. 172)
partly credit partially believe in
presage foretell the future
former ensign foremost banner or standard

BRUTUS O, if thou wert the noblest of thy strain,
        Young man, thou couldst not die more honourable.   60
CASSIUS A peevish schoolboy, worthless of such honour,
        Joined with a masker and a reveller!
ANTONY Old Cassius still!
OCTAVIUS   Come, Antony, away!
        Defiance, traitors, hurl we in your teeth.
        If you dare fight today, come to the field;   65
        If not, when you have stomachs.
                  Exeunt Octavius, Antony, and army
CASSIUS Why now blow wind, swell billow, and swim bark!
        The storm is up, and all is on the hazard.
BRUTUS Ho, Lucilius, hark, a word with you.
        Lucilius and Messala stand forth
LUCILIUS   My lord.
        [Brutus speaks apart to Lucilius]
CASSIUS Messala!
MESSALA   What says my general?
CASSIUS   Messala,   70
        This is my birthday, as this very day
        Was Cassius born. Give me thy hand, Messala.
        Be thou my witness that against my will
        (As Pompey was) am I compelled to set
        Upon one battle all our liberties.   75
        You know that I held Epicurus strong
        And his opinion. Now I change my mind
        And partly credit things that do presage.
        Coming from Sardis, on our former ensign
        Two mighty eagles fell, and there they perched,   80
        Gorging and feeding from our soldiers' hands,
        Who to Philippi here consorted us.
        This morning are they fled away and gone,
        And in their steads do ravens, crows, and kites
        Fly o'er our heads and downward look on us   85
        As we were sickly prey. Their shadows seem
        A canopy most fatal under which
        Our army lies, ready to give up the ghost.
MESSALA Believe not so.

Cassius is in high spirits despite the omens. He persuades Brutus to prefer suicide to captivity. They part in friendship and readiness for whatever the future holds.

---

1 Can you guess who is speaking? (in groups of four)

Talk together about all the differences between Cassius' and Brutus' language that we find in the play: lines 103–15 of Act 1 Scene 3 are typical of Cassius; lines 12–21 of Act 2 Scene 1 are typical of Brutus.

Two of you now close your eyes. The other two read aloud lines 92–125 of Act 5 Scene 1, but omitting any mention of the names Brutus and Cassius. After the reading, guess who read Cassius, who Brutus, and give your reasons. Is it easy to tell who is who at this point?

2 Brutus, the 'noble Roman' (in pairs)

Although he is a Roman, Brutus seems in lines 100–7 to be feeling his way towards the Christian doctrine condemning suicide. His words seem prophetic, but after a pause for thought at line 109 he decides to take the noble Roman's way out and kill himself if he is defeated.

Talk together about Brutus' pause for thought and run through everything that must have gone through his mind in that moment before he said 'No, Cassius, no'.

3 Inspiring the troops (individually or in pairs)

Compose a 'pep talk' to be delivered just before the battle by one of the four generals. Make sure it is characteristic of that leader. Sum up in stirring phrases what the soldiers are fighting for.

4 Farewells (in pairs)

Practise different ways of speaking lines 115–21 and then staging Brutus and Cassius' parting at line 125. Which of your interpretations do you find most effective and why?

The gods . . . friendly   may the gods today remain on our side
still incertain   always uncertain
philosophy   (i.e. Stoicism, which advocated suicide)
Cato   Portia's father, who took his own life (see also p. 56)

prevent / The time of life   end one's life before the proper time
stay the providence   wait for the decision
led in triumph   (as a humiliated captive)

CASSIUS   I but believe it partly,
        For I am fresh of spirit and resolved   90
        To meet all perils very constantly.
BRUTUS Even so, Lucilius. [*Advancing*]
CASSIUS   Now, most noble Brutus,
        The gods today stand friendly that we may,
        Lovers in peace, lead on our days to age!   95
        But since the affairs of men rests still incertain,
        Let's reason with the worst that may befall.
        If we do lose this battle, then is this
        The very last time we shall speak together.
        What are you then determinèd to do?   100
BRUTUS Even by the rule of that philosophy
        By which I did blame Cato for the death
        Which he did give himself – I know not how,
        But I do find it cowardly and vile,
        For fear of what might fall, so to prevent   105
        The time of life – arming myself with patience
        To stay the providence of some high powers
        That govern us below.
CASSIUS   Then if we lose this battle,
        You are contented to be led in triumph
        Through the streets of Rome?   110
BRUTUS No, Cassius, no. Think not, thou noble Roman,
        That ever Brutus will go bound to Rome:
        He bears too great a mind. But this same day
        Must end that work the Ides of March begun.
        And whether we shall meet again I know not,   115
        Therefore our everlasting farewell take:
        For ever and for ever, farewell, Cassius!
        If we do meet again, why, we shall smile;
        If not, why then this parting was well made.
CASSIUS For ever and for ever, farewell, Brutus!   120
        If we do meet again, we'll smile indeed;
        If not, 'tis true this parting was well made.
BRUTUS Why then, lead on. O, that a man might know
        The end of this day's business ere it come!
        But it sufficeth that the day will end,   125
        And then the end is known. Come ho, away!

                                           Exeunt

Battle. As Octavius weakens, Brutus orders all his troops to attack. On another part of the battlefield, Cassius reports that his soldiers have fled. Flee, says Pindarus, Antony is in our camp.

---

1 'Over now to our reporter at Philippi' (groups of four)

War reporters on television tell us about:

- what's happening
- the commander's overall strategy
- the state of morale, from general to footsoldier.

Devise a short national news report about the events of Philippi described opposite. Use reporters' commentary, (improvised) news-reel, maps and interviews.

2 Theatre of war (in large groups)

The stage direction 'Alarum' means that the events in this scene are preceded by a loud battle noise of drums, trumpets, voices and clashing weapons offstage. How can the battle be shown and heard on stage?

a Start at Act 5 Scene 1, line 119, and use all resources available to make the sound effects that change scenes up to Act 5 Scene 3, line 4. Each scene has a different mood, and your effects must make this clear. The right volume and quality of noise take careful planning.

b While some work out sound effects, others work on the staging. Either restrict yourself to the four named characters, or bring on a host of soldiers. Have the whole field of battle in mind when you plot entries and exits. Ensure that you show their contrasting moods: thoughtful, joyful, fearful, dejected, fast, slow – or whatever you feel is appropriate.

This takes careful organisation, but will tell you a great deal about Shakespeare's stagecraft. You could plan it in the classroom and then act it out in a larger space.

Alarum sounds of battle (see Activity 2 above)
bills written orders
on the other side (i.e. Cassius' wing of the battle formation)
cold . . . in Octavio's wing low spirits in Octavius' troops

sudden push . . . overthrow a sudden attack will beat them
the villains fly (i.e. his own troops are running away)
ensign standard-bearer
fell to spoil began plundering and looting

Act 5 Scene 2
The battlefield at Philippi

Alarum. Enter BRUTUS *and Messala*

BRUTUS Ride, ride, Messala, ride, and give these bills
    Unto the legions on the other side.
        Loud alarum
    Let them set on at once, for I perceive
    But cold demeanour in Octavio's wing,
    And sudden push gives them the overthrow.   5
    Ride, ride, Messala, let them all come down.

                                          Exeunt

Act 5 Scene 3
A high place overlooking the battlefield at Philippi

Alarums. Enter CASSIUS *and* TITINIUS

CASSIUS O, look, Titinius, look, the villains fly!
    Myself have to mine own turned enemy.
    This ensign here of mine was turning back;
    I slew the coward and did take it from him.
TITINIUS O Cassius, Brutus gave the word too early,   5
    Who, having some advantage on Octavius,
    Took it too eagerly. His soldiers fell to spoil
    Whilst we by Antony are all enclosed.

            Enter PINDARUS

PINDARUS Fly further off, my lord, fly further off!
    Mark Antony is in your tents, my lord,   10
    Fly therefore, noble Cassius, fly far off.
CASSIUS This hill is far enough. Look, look, Titinius,
    Are those my tents where I perceive the fire?

Titinius leaves, on Cassius' orders. Pindarus reports that Titinius has been captured. Cassius decides on suicide and orders Pindarus to kill him. Pindarus obeys his command.

1 Snapshots of Cassius (in pairs)

Cassius' life has come full circle. It is his birthday:

> This day I breathèd first, time is come round
> And where I did begin there shall I end

a Plutarch describes Cassius as a 'choleric' (angry, hot-tempered) man, with a personal hatred of Caesar, who 'even from his cradle, could not abide any manner of tyrants'. But little else is known of the historical Cassius. What might the life of such a man have been like?

Draw a big circle with Cassius' first and last day of life at 12 o'clock. Imagine how he spent his life up to the start of the play. Make a pie chart of his fifty-five years, labelling each section with detailed notes.

b Cassius orders his loyal servant Pindarus to kill him (ironically with the sword that had previously killed Caesar). One of you reads Cassius' death speech (lines 33–46). The other is Pindarus.

Work together on staging an effective end to Cassius' life. Finish the presentation with a tableau which 'freezes' momentarily at the instant of death.

2 Pindarus – grief and joy

Pindarus is consumed with conflicting feelings: of guilt as he kills his master and of ecstasy at Cassius releasing him from slavery so he can begin a new life 'Where never Roman shall take note of him' (line 50).

Pindarus does not appear again in the play. Write his thoughts as he flees (line 50). What is his 'non-Roman' view of recent events?

---

even with a thought as quick as a thought
thick weak, dim
thou not'st you observe, see
is run his compass has come full circle

on the spur riding hard
light dismount
ta'en taken, captured
Parthia (modern-day Iran/Iraq)
I swore thee I made you promise
search probe, penetrate

TITINIUS They are, my lord.

CASSIUS   Titinius, if thou lovest me,
         Mount thou my horse and hide thy spurs in him   15
         Till he have brought thee up to yonder troops
         And here again that I may rest assured
         Whether yond troops are friend or enemy.

TITINIUS I will be here again even with a thought.   *Exit*

CASSIUS Go, Pindarus, get higher on that hill,   20
         My sight was ever thick: regard Titinius
         And tell me what thou not'st about the field.
                    [*Pindarus goes up*]
         This day I breathèd first, time is come round
         And where I did begin there shall I end:
         My life is run his compass. Sirrah, what news?   25

PINDARUS (*Above*) O my lord!

CASSIUS What news?

PINDARUS Titinius is enclosèd round about
         With horsemen that make to him on the spur,
         Yet he spurs on. Now they are almost on him.   30
         Now Titinius – Now some light; O, he lights too.
         He's ta'en.
                    (*Shout*)
              And hark, they shout for joy.

CASSIUS Come down, behold no more.
         O, coward that I am to live so long
         To see my best friend ta'en before my face.   35
                    Pindarus [*descends*]
         Come hither, sirrah.
         In Parthia did I take thee prisoner,
         And then I swore thee, saving of thy life,
         That whatsoever I did bid thee do
         Thou shouldst attempt it. Come now, keep thine oath.   40
         Now be a freeman, and with this good sword,
         That ran through Caesar's bowels, search this bosom.
         Stand not to answer; here, take thou the hilts
         And when my face is covered, as 'tis now,
         Guide thou the sword.
                    [*Pindarus stabs him*]
                    Caesar, thou art revenged   45
         Even with the sword that killed thee.   [*Dies*]

Pindarus flees. Messala and Titinius enter with news of Brutus' success over
Octavius. They hope to cheer Cassius but find him dead.

1 The end of the Republic (in groups of four or five)

After five hundred years the Republic is finished. Like millions of
persecuted, defeated or outlawed people in history – Jews in Nazi
Germany, Vietnamese boat people – Republicans anywhere in the
Empire realise that life as they knew it is over. Pindarus flees, Messala
will fight on, Titinius will kill himself.

- Lines 60–4 are Titinius' lament for the Republic. Take a line each
  and keep repeating it, building your lament like a piece of music.
  Speaking the verses in any order, start softly and chime your line
  into the ensemble of voices sparingly, then increase in volume and
  frequency as grief deepens. Savour the sadness of the words, which
  reach the listener as a collage of broken phrases.
- Lines 60–4 are also a lament for Cassius, showing that he inspired
  feelings of admiration and respect amongst his followers. Discuss
  how these lines fit with your earlier impressions of Cassius. Is
  Messala right to claim that 'Mistrust of good success' (looking on
  the dark side of things) was responsible for his downfall?

2 Error comes to life (individually or in small groups)

Cassius has made a fatal error. The battle is not yet lost. Titinius
was not captured but given a 'wreath of victory' (line 82). **Personification** is the presenting of ideas or things as if they were human.
Rumour actually came on stage in Shakespeare's *King Henry IV
Part 2*, in the guise of a man with tongues sewn all over his costume.
In lines 66–71 Messala creates a personification of Error, describes
its nature and even how it was born.

Make up your own story about this 'strange being' called Error.
Design a costume for Error to illustrate your story.

Durst I had I dared to	**mother** (i.e. the person who has the
change exchange, tit for tat	mistaken thoughts)
Mistrust of doubts about	**engendered** conceived
apt thoughts impressionable minds	

PINDARUS So I am free, yet would not so have been
          Durst I have done my will. O Cassius,
          Far from this country Pindarus shall run,
          Where never Roman shall take note of him.   *[Exit]*   50

Enter TITINIUS *and* MESSALA

MESSALA It is but change, Titinius, for Octavius
          Is overthrown by noble Brutus' power,
          As Cassius' legions are by Antony.
TITINIUS These tidings will well comfort Cassius.
MESSALA Where did you leave him?
TITINIUS   All disconsolate,   55
          With Pindarus his bondman, on this hill.
MESSALA Is not that he that lies upon the ground?
TITINIUS He lies not like the living. O my heart!
MESSALA Is not that he?
TITINIUS   No, this was he, Messala,
          But Cassius is no more. O setting sun,   60
          As in thy red rays thou dost sink to night,
          So in his red blood Cassius' day is set.
          The sun of Rome is set. Our day is gone,
          Clouds, dews, and dangers come. Our deeds are done.
          Mistrust of my success hath done this deed.   65
MESSALA Mistrust of good success hath done this deed.
          O hateful error, melancholy's child,
          Why dost thou show to the apt thoughts of men
          The things that are not? O error, soon conceived,
          Thou never com'st unto a happy birth   70
          But kill'st the mother that engendered thee.
TITINIUS What, Pindarus? Where art thou, Pindarus?
MESSALA Seek him, Titinius, whilst I go to meet
          The noble Brutus, thrusting this report
          Into his ears. I may say 'thrusting' it,   75
          For piercing steel and darts envenomèd
          Shall be as welcome to the ears of Brutus
          As tidings of this sight.
TITINIUS   Hie you, Messala,
          And I will seek for Pindarus the while.

                                 [Exit Messala]

Titinius places a victory wreath on Cassius' head, then loyally kills himself. Brutus and others enter and mourn the two dead men. Brutus orders his fellow Romans to fight on.

---

1 Seeing is believing (individually or in pairs)

Pindarus first got it wrong. Titinius was not captured by the enemy (which was what Pindarus 'saw', lines 28–30), but greeted by welcoming comrades. The victory garland sent by Brutus now becomes Cassius' funeral wreath. Titinius mourns that Cassius 'misconstrued everything'.

Head up two columns with 'Brutus' and 'Cassius' and fill them in with details about how each character has misinterpreted or misjudged what they have 'seen' during the course of the whole play.

2 I am Cassius' sword

Weapons can be objects of reverence and exquisite craftsmanship. In stories they often have magical powers. Shakespeare's characters often swear on, or by, their swords. Cassius introduces us to his dagger/sword in Act 1 Scene 3, line 89: 'I know where I will wear this dagger then: / Cassius from bondage will deliver Cassius.' He stabs Caesar with it (Act 3 Scene 1, line 76) and invites Brutus to kill him with it (Act 4 Scene 3, line 100). By the time we reach this scene it has a life of its own. In line 45 Cassius asks Pindarus to 'Guide thou the sword'; in line 90 it is told to 'find Titinius' heart'; in lines 94–6 Brutus imagines the dead Caesar wields it 'and turns our swords / In our own proper entrails'.

Gather these thoughts into a poem that starts 'I am Cassius' sword'.

3 Brutus' tribute (in pairs)

Take turns to read aloud Brutus' lines 98–110. Work out ways to balance the deeply grieving respect he gives to his two dead companions with the need to rouse and inspire the survivors for one last victory push.

---

brave Cassius   noble Cassius
misconstrued   misinterpreted (see
 Activity 1 above)
hold thee   wait a moment
regarded   honoured

a Roman's part   how a Roman should
 die (i.e. by suicide)
own proper   very own
Look whe'er   see how
Thasos   island near Philippi
discomfort us   dishearten our troops

Why didst thou send me forth, brave Cassius?   80
Did I not meet thy friends? And did not they
Put on my brows this wreath of victory
And bid me give it thee? Didst thou not hear their shouts?
Alas, thou hast misconstrued everything.
But hold thee, take this garland on thy brow;   85
Thy Brutus bid me give it thee, and I
Will do his bidding. Brutus, come apace,
And see how I regarded Caius Cassius.
By your leave, gods! – This is a Roman's part.
Come, Cassius' sword, and find Titinius' heart.   *Dies*   90

Alarum. Enter BRUTUS, MESSALA, YOUNG CATO, *Strato, Volumnius,*
and Lucilius, [*Labeo, and Flavius*]

BRUTUS Where, where, Messala, doth his body lie?
MESSALA Lo yonder, and Titinius mourning it.
BRUTUS Titinius' face is upward.
CATO   He is slain.
BRUTUS O Julius Caesar, thou art mighty yet,
        Thy spirit walks abroad and turns our swords   95
        In our own proper entrails.
                        Low alarums
CATO   Brave Titinius!
        Look whe'er he have not crowned dead Cassius.
BRUTUS Are yet two Romans living such as these?
        The last of all the Romans, fare thee well!
        It is impossible that ever Rome   100
        Should breed thy fellow. Friends, I owe mo tears
        To this dead man than you shall see me pay.
        I shall find time, Cassius, I shall find time.
        Come therefore and to Thasos send his body;
        His funerals shall not be in our camp   105
        Lest it discomfort us. Lucilius, come,
        And come, young Cato, let us to the field.
        Labeo and Flavio, set our battles on.
        'Tis three o'clock, and, Romans, yet ere night
        We shall try fortune in a second fight.   110
                                            Exeunt

Battle. Brutus encourages his troops, then leaves. Left behind, Cato is killed in combat and Lucilius (posing as Brutus) captured. Lucilius drops his pretence when Antony enters.

---

1 Swashbucklers (in small groups)

Young men used to swagger in the streets of Elizabethan London, shouting and banging their swords on their 'bucklers' (little shields) as a general challenge to fight. The authorities thought them a public menace. It is reported that some women found them sexy.

Work lines 4–8 into something like a chant. Then try it with your own name, and compose your own tag along the lines of 'A foe to tyrants, and my country's friend'.

2 Brutus' men

Work out what is happening in the scene and what it tells us about Brutus and his men (especially Cato and Lucilius). In particular, think why Lucilius pretends to be Brutus and why Antony decides to 'Give him all kindness' when he recognises that Lucilius is not Brutus.

Plan a staging of the scene to make good sense of every line.

3 Glorious war (in groups of eight)

This is the only actual fight called for by a stage direction so it must be performed well on stage. Display fighting was a popular entertainment in Elizabethan times.

Plan, in slow motion, how you would stage the fight from *Enter soldiers* to *Young Cato is slain*. Your fight should be convincing, but never dangerous. The golden rule of stage-fighting is *safety first*!

Yet keep going!
What bastard doth not? who is of such low parentage that he does not (want to keep fighting)?

Only I yield to die (i.e. I will die before I surrender)
There is . . . straight There is good reason for you to kill me quickly (i.e. because I am Brutus)

Act 5 Scene 4
The battlefield at Philippi

Alarum. Enter BRUTUS, *Messala,* [YOUNG] CATO, LUCILIUS,
and Flavius, [Labeo]

BRUTUS Yet, countrymen, O, yet hold up your heads!
               [Exit with Messala, Flavius, and Labeo]
CATO What bastard doth not? Who will go with me?
    I will proclaim my name about the field.
    I am the son of Marcus Cato, ho!
    A foe to tyrants, and my country's friend.   5
    I am the son of Marcus Cato, ho!

            Enter SOLDIERS *and fight*

LUCILIUS And I am Brutus, Marcus Brutus, I,
    Brutus, my country's friend. Know me for Brutus!
           [Young Cato is slain]
    O young and noble Cato, art thou down?
    Why, now thou diest as bravely as Titinius   10
    And mayst be honoured, being Cato's son.
1 SOLDIER Yield, or thou diest.
LUCILIUS   Only I yield to die.
    There is so much that thou wilt kill me straight.
    Kill Brutus and be honoured in his death.
1 SOLDIER We must not. A noble prisoner!   15

            Enter ANTONY

2 SOLDIER Room ho! Tell Antony, Brutus is ta'en.
1 SOLDIER I'll tell the news. Here comes the general.
    Brutus is ta'en, Brutus is ta'en, my lord!
ANTONY Where is he?
LUCILIUS Safe, Antony, Brutus is safe enough.   20
    I dare assure thee that no enemy
    Shall ever take alive the noble Brutus.
    The gods defend him from so great a shame!
    When you do find him, or alive or dead,
    He will be found like Brutus, like himself.   25

Antony gives safe custody to Lucilius and sends for word of Brutus. Brutus and
followers enter and rest. Separately and secretly he asks them to kill him.

---

1 What are Antony's motives? (in small groups)

Far from being angry at Lucilius' attempt to impersonate Brutus,
Antony treats him with the greatest respect and kindness (Act 5
Scene 4, lines 26–9). Discuss the different motives Antony might
have for doing this.

2 Contrasts of war (in large groups)

Scene 4 is all about violence, glory and action. Scene 5 opens peace-
fully and quietly. Some dialogue is a whisper, so quiet you can't hear
it. Strato falls asleep. But as the voice of battle steadily grows in
volume, Brutus' plea for help in his suicide becomes urgent.

Bring out these contrasts by making a tape recording of the script
from the start of Act 5 Scene 4 to Act 5 Scene 5, line 57. Rehearse
and co-ordinate sound effects and dialogue very carefully.

3 'Poor remains of friends' (in groups of four or five)

Who are Brutus' four 'poor remains of friends' (Dardanio, Clitus,
Strato and Volumnius)? We have never before seen them in the play.
'Hot seat' each friend. To do this, ask the character all the questions
you can think of about who he is. Your questions should help each
'friend' think of answers, which could be made up using a combina-
tion of their own imagination and knowledge of the play.

If you are one of the people being hot-seated, you may decide
for example that your character had an important behind-the-scenes
part to play which nobody ever knew about!

---

showed the torchlight   gave the
signal when he reached Cassius'
camp
or ta'en or slain   either captured or
killed

deed in fashion   popular thing to do at
the moment
Now is . . . vessel full of grief   the
noble [Brutus] is like a jug brimful with
sad tears
several   separate

ANTONY This is not Brutus, friend, but, I assure you,
            A prize no less in worth. Keep this man safe,
            Give him all kindness. I had rather have
            Such men my friends than enemies. Go on,
            And see whe'er Brutus be alive or dead,   30
            And bring us word unto Octavius' tent
            How everything is chanced.

Exeunt

Act 5 Scene 5
A rocky place near the battlefield at Philippi

Enter BRUTUS, DARDANIUS, CLITUS, STRATO, and VOLUMNIUS

BRUTUS Come, poor remains of friends, rest on this rock.
CLITUS Statilius showed the torchlight but, my lord,
            He came not back. He is or ta'en or slain.
BRUTUS Sit thee down, Clitus. Slaying is the word,
            It is a deed in fashion. Hark thee, Clitus. [*Whispering*]   5
CLITUS What, I, my lord? No, not for all the world.
BRUTUS Peace then, no words.
CLITUS   I'll rather kill myself.
BRUTUS Hark thee, Dardanius. [*Whispers*]
DARDANIUS   Shall I do such a deed?
CLITUS O Dardanius!
DARDANIUS O Clitus!   10
CLITUS What ill request did Brutus make to thee?
DARDANIUS To kill him, Clitus. Look, he meditates.
CLITUS Now is that noble vessel full of grief,
            That it runs over even at his eyes.
BRUTUS Come hither, good Volumnius, list a word.   15
VOLUMNIUS What says my lord?
BRUTUS   Why, this, Volumnius:
            The ghost of Caesar hath appeared to me
            Two several times by night, at Sardis once
            And this last night here in Philippi fields.
            I know my hour is come.
VOLUMNIUS   Not so, my lord.   20

Volumnius refuses to aid Brutus' suicide. Brutus bids farewell to his friends. He urges them to fly. But he detains Strato, who helps Brutus to take his own life.

1 'Brutus' tongue' (in groups of five)

In taking his own life Brutus is his own biographer. He writes himself a noble death: 'Brutus' tongue / Hath almost ended his life's history'. Volumnius, an old school friend, disagrees with Brutus twice, but as usual we hear only Brutus' side of the argument.

To let Clitus, Dardanius and Volumnius give their point of view, delay Antony's approach and have them refuse to leave at line 43. Improvise what happens as they probe the wisdom and sincerity of Brutus' motives in committing suicide both now and in the future. Brutus and Strato defend his actions.

After your improvisation, see if you can read Brutus' part with more conviction and realism than before.

2 Brutus alone (in pairs)

Shakespeare deliberately increases Brutus' isolation as his death approaches. The increasing intensity of the 'alarums' (sounds of battle) suggests the Triumvirate's unstoppable advance. Brutus' last few friends flee until only Strato is left as a companion.

Rehearse and present Brutus' lines 50–1 in slow motion, ending with a freeze-frame, then talk with other pairs about the effects you have created. How adequately do Brutus' final words sum up the man himself?

3 Two suicides (in groups of three or four)

Imagine that the accounts of Cassius' death (Act 5 Scene 3, lines 1–46) and of Brutus' death (Act 5 Scene 5, lines 1–51) are printed side by side in the Roman newspapers.

• Write the newspaper reports.
• As a Roman family, talk over the similarities and differences and compare their nobility.

---

beat us to the pit driven us before them (like hunted animals into a pit)
vile conquest shameful victory

good respect good reputation
smatch trace, smack

BRUTUS   Nay, I am sure it is, Volumnius.
　　　　　Thou seest the world, Volumnius, how it goes:
　　　　　Our enemies have beat us to the pit.

Low alarums

　　　　　It is more worthy to leap in ourselves
　　　　　Than tarry till they push us. Good Volumnius,　　　　25
　　　　　Thou know'st that we two went to school together;
　　　　　Even for that our love of old, I prithee
　　　　　Hold thou my sword-hilts whilst I run on it.
VOLUMNIUS   That's not an office for a friend, my lord.

Alarum still

CLITUS   Fly, fly, my lord, there is no tarrying here.　　　　30
BRUTUS   Farewell to you, and you, and you, Volumnius.
　　　　　Strato, thou hast been all this while asleep:
　　　　　Farewell to thee too, Strato. Countrymen,
　　　　　My heart doth joy that yet in all my life
　　　　　I found no man but he was true to me.　　　　　　35
　　　　　I shall have glory by this losing day
　　　　　More than Octavius and Mark Antony
　　　　　By this vile conquest shall attain unto.
　　　　　So fare you well at once, for Brutus' tongue
　　　　　Hath almost ended his life's history.　　　　　　40
　　　　　Night hangs upon mine eyes, my bones would rest,
　　　　　That have but laboured to attain this hour.

Alarum. Cry within, 'Fly, fly, fly!'

CLITUS   Fly, my lord, fly!
BRUTUS　　　　　　　　Hence! I will follow.

[Exeunt Clitus, Dardanius, and Volumnius]

　　　　　I prithee, Strato, stay thou by thy lord.
　　　　　Thou art a fellow of a good respect,　　　　　　45
　　　　　Thy life hath had some smatch of honour in it.
　　　　　Hold then my sword and turn away thy face,
　　　　　While I do run upon it. Wilt thou, Strato?
STRATO   Give me your hand first. Fare you well, my lord.
BRUTUS   Farewell, good Strato.

[Runs on his sword]

　　　　　　　　　　Caesar, now be still,　　　　　　　50
　　　　　I killed not thee with half so good a will.　　*Dies*

To the sound of the retreating conspirators' trumpets, the triumvirs enter and accept Brutus' followers into their service. Antony honours Brutus as the only selfless conspirator.

---

1 Clemency – wisdom or folly? (in groups of four)

Octavius shows clemency (mercy) to all of Brutus' followers when he spares their lives. Julius Caesar also showed clemency to the followers of Pompey after he had defeated them. Among those same followers were Brutus and Cassius, who later assassinated the merciful Caesar.

Is Octavius making the same mistake as Caesar? Two of you take the part of Octavius. The others play advisers who are not happy with Octavius' decision. Debate who is right.

2 Brutus or Antony the hero? (in groups of five or six)

Antony's tribute to Brutus (lines 68–75) is fulsome in its praise of 'the noblest Roman of them all'. He singles out Brutus amongst the conspirators as not being driven by 'envy of great Caesar' but by a concern for the 'common good to all'.

Look at Antony's final lines in the play. Write a paragraph about their dramatic impact and what you think they add to your opinions of Brutus' character and Antony's. Which man is the greater hero?

3 Curtain! (in groups of about twelve)

When Octavius speaks the last words of the play, he unceremoniously (but tellingly) asserts his leadership and authority.

Many productions choose to suggest a possible irony in the ending. Caesar disposed of Pompey to become sole ruler of Rome, but will there now be a new power struggle between Antony and Octavius?

Present the play's closing moment as a tableau or freeze-frame which suggests just such a future hostility between the two victorious generals.

Retreat (on drums or trumpets)
entertain them take them into my service
prefer recommend
latest final
envy of enmity towards
a general . . . good to all an honest concern for the public good

made one of them joined them
mixed well balanced
virtue quality, excellence
use him treat him
part share out

Alarum. Retreat. Enter ANTONY, OCTAVIUS, MESSALA,
LUCILIUS, *and the army*

OCTAVIUS What man is that?

MESSALA My master's man. Strato, where is thy master?

STRATO Free from the bondage you are in, Messala.
       The conquerors can but make a fire of him: 55
       For Brutus only overcame himself,
       And no man else hath honour by his death.

LUCILIUS So Brutus should be found. I thank thee, Brutus,
       That thou hast proved Lucilius' saying true.

OCTAVIUS All that served Brutus I will entertain them.   60
       Fellow, wilt thou bestow thy time with me?

STRATO Ay, if Messala will prefer me to you.

OCTAVIUS Do so, good Messala.

MESSALA How died my master, Strato?

STRATO I held the sword, and he did run on it.   65

MESSALA Octavius, then take him to follow thee,
       That did the latest service to my master.

ANTONY This was the noblest Roman of them all:
       All the conspirators, save only he,
       Did that they did in envy of great Caesar.   70
       He only, in a general honest thought
       And common good to all, made one of them.
       His life was gentle, and the elements
       So mixed in him that Nature might stand up
       And say to all the world, 'This was a man!'   75

OCTAVIUS According to his virtue let us use him,
       With all respect and rites of burial.
       Within my tent his bones tonight shall lie,
       Most like a soldier, ordered honourably.
       So call the field to rest, and let's away   80
       To part the glories of this happy day.

Exeunt

Looking back at the play

1 What was the fighting about?

It is two years since Caesar's assassination, and both sides, Republicans and triumvirs, have been campaigning continuously against each other. Imagine that you are two surviving senators who have been fighting on opposing sides. You may even have known each other in the old days in Rome. So that you can make sense in your own mind of the hardship of the last two years, try to explain to your former enemy what it was that you were fighting for.

2 Press statement

In modern warfare, after a great victory the triumphant generals often meet the press, have their photographs taken and issue a press statement. Two people take the roles of Antony and Octavius, while the others prepare to be members of the press or television. Question the two leaders and get as much out of them as you can. Afterwards, write the press statement issued by the victors. (Antony and Octavius might decide to release separate statements.)

3 The story of the play

Now that you have finished reading *Julius Caesar*, look back to the colour photograph section on pages v–xii. Do those photographs tell the story of the play accurately? Would you have used the same spread of images or different ones? Are there any incidents or issues that have been omitted? Talk with a partner about these questions, and then produce your own storyboard for *Julius Caesar*.

4 Fifteen-minute version

Divide the class into five groups, each group taking one act of the play. You are going to produce a three-minute version of your chosen act, using only the words from the script itself. When you are ready, put each of the five acts together in turn; you have created a fifteen-minute version of the whole play.

As a variation, mime or perform each act in a different style (documentary investigation, soap opera, melodrama, and so on).

5 Cast the play

Imagine that you are a film director about to put together a new and ambitious version of *Julius Caesar*. Go through the list of characters on page 1, and choose the eight that you think are most important in the play. Decide which well-known film actors you would cast in each part – money no object! In each case, say what it is about that particular actor that makes you think they are right for the part.

6 Octavius – the new Caesar?

Octavius Caesar (standing, centre) speaks the final lines of the play. As a key member of the Triumvirate he has risen slickly to power. This is how one production presented him. How far do his appearance and demeanour match your own impressions of Julius Caesar's relative?

What is the play about?

Julius Caesar was probably written in 1599 and first performed in the same year on the stage of the Globe Theatre on London's Bankside. Although essentially a tragedy, it is also a history play dealing with politics and war. However, unlike most of Shakespeare's other history plays, it is not drawn from English history or from Tudor England's recent past.

Shakespeare's main source for his story of *Julius Caesar* is a text that he probably studied at school: Plutarch's *The Lives of the Noble Grecians and Romans*, translated into English by Thomas North in 1579. Shakespeare was probably particularly interested in Plutarch's *Lives* because it contained interesting, biographically detailed, rich and complex appreciations of famous people at the centre of historical events, rather than being simply a re-telling of the events. In addition Plutarch was drawn towards studies of power and the personal dilemmas faced by political leaders. All this made fertile source material for Shakespeare to shape and fashion in his own distinctive way. The changes that he made to Plutarch's historical account include:

- having Calpurnia present at the Lupercal festival; using Casca to report Caesar's three-time refusal of the crown (Act 1 Scene 2)
- adding Brutus' long soliloquy in Act 2 Scene 1
- having Caesar reject Artemidorus' written warning about the conspiracy (Act 2 Scene 3 and Act 3 Scene 1)
- showing the assassins ritually bathing their arms in Caesar's blood (Act 3 Scene 1)
- adjusting the sequence of events so Antony's funeral oration follows directly after Brutus' speech of explanation to the Roman people; having Antony read out the details of Caesar's will (Act 3 Scene 2)

- ◆ Choose one of the 'changes' listed above. Write a paragraph discussing what the play gains from the alteration that Shakespeare made.

Politics

The feeling that great events are happening, events that will shape all subsequent history, is unmistakably present. This may be ancient history, but it is told with racy vitality. How is this achieved?

Probably by its mixture of old and new. Shakespeare's Rome owes much to Tudor London – its people even dress in doublets – but it is spiced by specifically pre-Christian superstition and cruelty such as the sacrifice of animals and the mob slaughter of the poet Cinna. The pagan world had not yet learned of the teaching of Jesus Christ, though intelligent and educated men like Cicero had brought it 'civilisation' and 'culture'.

An advantage of setting his play in ancient Rome was that Shakespeare could present a debate about authority without fear of offending Queen Elizabeth and her government or arousing religious controversy. Although the fact that the conspirators' attempt to save the Roman Republic actually failed was no doubt conveniently reassuring to the Tudor authorities, Caesar's assassination would have been an uncomfortable reminder to Elizabethans of the many attempts on the life of the queen (her Jewish physician was executed for allegedly trying to poison her). Similarly, some Elizabethans believed the queen's power, like Caesar's, to be growing too great. Others were as concerned as the ancient Romans about the threat of political upheaval and civil war when their ageing and childless queen finally died.

Themes in *Julius Caesar*

Another way of looking at the play is to discuss its themes. Themes are ideas or issues or topics that recur throughout the play (rather like repeated melodies in a piece of music). They suggest that Shakespeare was preoccupied by particular ideas as he wrote, and sought to explore them through a drama that would entertain his audiences – and make them think. Such major themes include: death; sickness and disease; public versus private; love and friendship.

Death

The idea of death and its physical representation runs through the play:

- Flavius and Murellus are killed for removing the decorations from Caesar's statues (Act 1 Scene 2).
- Cassius frequently mentions the possibility of suicide. Brutus resolves to kill Caesar: 'It must be by his death' (Act 2 Scene 1).
- After the frenzied stabbing of Caesar, his bloodied body is vividly present on stage and used to rouse the crowd to an avenging fury against the 'traitors' who killed him (Act 3 Scene 2).

- The innocent poet Cinna is pointlessly killed by the Roman mob (Act 3 Scene 3).
- Antony coolly approves the execution of his nephew as the Triumvirate seek to establish control of Rome (Act 4 Scene 1).
- Portia kills herself; Caesar's ghost appears to Brutus (Act 4 Scene 3).
- Pindarus helps Cassius to commit suicide; Titinius, displaying loyalty to Cassius, takes his own life (Act 5 Scene 3).
- Strato helps Brutus to kill himself (Act 5 Scene 5).

◆ Use the ideas above, and any of your own, to write a short essay on the importance of death in *Julius Caesar*.

Sickness and disease

Disease and infection were rife in Elizabethan England. Unpleasant sexual diseases and, particularly, the bubonic plague were a constant threat, and epidemics were frequent. *Julius Caesar* contains many references to sickness and ill-health. When Murellus urges the common people to 'Pray to the gods to intermit [prevent] the plague' his words carry a strong contemporary resonance.

Caesar's human frailty is highlighted by focusing on his deafness and his epilepsy. Caesar has also, like Elizabeth I, been unable to beget an heir (Calpurnia is attending the Lupercal ceremony in an attempt to 'cure' her infertility). Cassius has poor eyesight.

Shakespeare frequently connects the sickness of the body with that of the mind. In Act 2 Scene 1 Portia asks 'Is Brutus sick?' when she witnesses his troubled sleeplessness in 'the vile contagion of the night' and concludes that her husband has 'some sick offence within [his] mind'; Ligarius' sickness is cured when he joins the conspiracy against Caesar; and to Brutus the assassination is 'A piece of work that will make sick men whole'.

◆ Research the prevalence of sickness and disease in Elizabethan England and prepare a short presentation to the class on how vulnerable and frightened Shakespeare's audiences would have been.

Public versus private

Many aspects of the play explore the dramatic tension between public and private events. At its heart are the big 'set-piece' public scenes involving Caesar's assassination and the speeches by Brutus and Antony to the Roman crowd after Caesar's death. The play begins (Act 1 Scene 2) with the common people applauding Caesar's victory over Pompey, then shows the Lupercal festival where Antony is reported as offering a crown to Caesar three times; Caesar's epileptic fit even happens publicly 'in the market-place'.

After the murder the play focuses increasingly on the nationwide repercussions of Caesar's assassination as mob violence drives Brutus and Cassius from Rome and precipitates civil war. The play's final scenes show faction fighting against faction and destruction and disorder on a grand scale. Shakespeare even includes a self-indulgent reference by Cassius to the way in which future actors will re-enact 'our lofty scene'.

Yet the play is also keen to explore issues at an individual 'private' level. There is Cassius' expression of his personal hatred of Caesar (Act 1 Scene 3); Brutus' agonised soliloquy in his orchard (Act 2 Scene 1); the domestic scenes showing Portia with Brutus and Calpurnia with Caesar (Act 2 Scenes 1 and 2); the presentation of Caesar's human frailties against his grand public self-confidence (Act 2 Scene 2); Antony's private outpourings of grief ('O, pardon me, thou bleeding piece of earth') and revenge ('Now let it work. Mischief, thou art afoot') which immediately follow his apparently equally sincere public speeches to the conspirators and the Roman crowd (Act 3 Scenes 1 and 2); and Brutus and Cassius' private reconciliation (Act 4 Scene 3).

♦ Write an analysis of one scene in the play in which you think Shakespeare skilfully explores the tension between 'public' and 'private'.

Love and friendship

The nature of the male friendships presented in the play reflects Elizabethan values. The main male characters express deep and loyal affection for each other. Antony's friendship and admiration for Caesar are first suggested in Act 1 and given full dramatic play in Act 3 after Caesar's murder: 'Thou art the ruins of the noblest man / That ever lived in the tide of times'. Brutus and Cassius share a similarly powerful friendship, even though they are not like-minded characters. In Act 4 Scene 3 after their bitter quarrel, Shakespeare stresses the importance of their reconciliation as Cassius declares 'I cannot drink too much of Brutus' love.' Brutus also inspires love and affection in Portia, his servant Lucius and his friends. This makes Brutus' betrayal of his friend Caesar all the more treacherous. Caesar's dying words in Act 3 Scene 1 ('*Et tu, Brute?* [Even you, Brutus?] – Then fall, Caesar!') express his disbelief at what is happening. Brutus' traitorous betrayal is almost as fatal to Caesar as the conspirators' savage stab wounds.

In striking contrast, the young and inexperienced Octavius is portrayed in Acts 4 and 5 as controlled, detached and calculating. Shakespeare will develop this coldly formidable, efficient character in much greater detail in his later play *Antony and Cleopatra*.

◆ Working in small groups, make a list of the main characters. For each write a short paragraph about their attitudes to love and friendship.

Blood

Both images and actual representations of blood abound in the play. In the opening scene the common people champion Caesar 'over Pompey's blood'. Antony speaks of how Pompey's statue ran with blood as Caesar fell dead at its base. Brutus agonises about behaving like a 'butcher' during the assassination and is cautious about killing Antony lest their 'course will seem too bloody'. After the murder the conspirators smear their arms with Caesar's blood. Portia wounds herself to prove her devotion to Brutus. Calpurnia dreams of clouds which 'drizzled blood' and of her husband's statue which 'Did run pure blood'. As Antony shakes the hand of each conspirator his own is smeared with Caesar's blood. During his funeral oration Antony makes moving use of Caesar's bloodied robe and conjures up powerful images of Caesar's blood: 'Caesar's wounds, poor, poor, dumb mouths'.

As the references to blood diminish after Act 3, we are reminded that it is Caesar's spirit rather than his body that will now dominate events. Only when Brutus dies can he declare: 'Caesar, now be still'.

◆ Collect all the references to blood in the play. Display your findings as a striking, visual presentation.

The Roman world

This alphabetical section provides details about some of the Roman people, places and customs that Shakespeare incorporated into his play.

Aeneas (see p. 16) was a Trojan hero, the son of Anchises and the goddess Venus. Aeneas' journey from Troy (retold in Virgil's epic poem *The Aeneid*) led to the founding of the city that was to become Rome.

Armies in Rome were privately owned. They were paid for by individuals who sometimes put them at the service of the state.

♦ Research the equipment and fighting techniques of the Roman soldier, and then suggest ways of using some of your information to devise suitable costumes for a stage production.

Augurers (see p. 50). Any decision of importance was referred to the augurers, who had various ways of determining the will of the gods and deciding whether it was lucky or unlucky to proceed on that day. Sometimes (see **Sacrifice** below) a live animal was cut open and its insides studied. In Act 2 Scene 1, line 200, Cassius refers to Caesar's belief in the power of augurers, omens and dreams, which he fears will prevent him from going to the Capitol and thereby ruin the conspirators' plans.

♦ Look back at Act 2 Scene 2, lines 1–107, where Caesar debates whether to go to the Capitol. Describe how Shakespeare has used dreams, omens and auguries to add to the scene's dramatic tension.

Cicero (106–43 BC) (see p. 20) was the leading orator of his day. His writings were intensely studied in Elizabethan schools. His style was held up as the ideal model for students. His essays, letters and imaginary conversations between historical figures popularised the ideas of Greek philosophers, presenting them in a pleasurable and accessible style.

♦ Look back at Cicero's part in the play (Act 1 Scenes 2 and 3). Suggest ways in which an actor might portray something of the historical Cicero in the way he performs his role.

The city of Rome was built around two locations. The **forum** was the central area where commerce and the administration of justice were focused. The **Capitol** (the walled part of ancient Rome), on one of its seven hills, was the political and religious centre of the Roman Empire.

◆ Research what ancient Rome looked like. Choose one scene from the play and design the set and costumes for that scene. Suggest ways of bringing out the atmosphere of ancient Rome.

Colossus (see p. 18) was a giant statue of the Greek god Apollo that bestrode the harbour entrance to the Greek island of Rhodes. Over 30 metres high (the tallest statue of its time), it was known as one of the seven wonders of the ancient world.

Cynics (see p. 126) believed primarily in two key principles: that the individual was responsible for their own morality and that a person's mental determination ('will') was all-important. They rejected the social values of the time, preached the avoidance of pleasure and denied social relationships. **Cynicism** was the forerunner of **Stoicism** (see below).

Epicurus (see p. 144) was a Greek philosopher who founded **Epicureanism**. He believed that seeking simple and modest pleasures was the route to tranquillity and freedom from fear.

Honour (see also **Suicide** below) in ancient times and in Shakespeare's day was not the vague concept it is today. Aristotle, a famous ancient Greek philosopher, explained how the **magnanimous man** (the perfect ruler) made public honour his 'chief concern'.

◆ Discuss how Shakespeare explores the theme of honour in the play. Look closely at what Brutus and Cassius say about it (e.g. in Act 1 Scene 2 and Act 3 Scene 2) and how they approach their deaths. What does 'honour' mean to them?

The Lupercal (see p. 10) was originally a farming festival held on 15 February to ward wolves off the newborn lambs and kids in the flocks. Later it was adopted by the city of Rome to ward off evil spirits. Just as the billygoats brought fertility to the flocks, barren women thought the flick of a goatskin flail would enable them to have children.

Octavius Caesar (63 BC – AD 14), grand-nephew to Julius Caesar, achieved high office at an early age. Caesar treated him as his heir. After Caesar's assassination (as seen in the play) Octavius establishes the Second Triumvirate with Antony and Lepidus, but later (as seen in *Antony and Cleopatra*) Lepidus is disposed of, and then Octavius and Antony quarrel and battle with each other. Octavius wins and becomes sole ruler of the Roman Empire, with the title of Emperor Caesar Augustus.

Pompey (106–48 BC) (see p. 8) was, like Caesar, a very popular general; both were members of the First Triumvirate (with Crassus). He married Caesar's daughter Julia. Pompey stayed at home, while Caesar campaigned in Europe, becoming increasingly powerful. When Caesar returned and declared himself dictator, Pompey fled and was finally murdered. Shakespeare's *Julius Caesar* opens after Caesar has wiped out a final pocket of resistance headed by Pompey's sons.

Proscription (see p. 112) was the imposition of the death penalty; three hundred out of nine hundred senators were executed along with two hundred *equites* (aristocrats).

Sacrifice of animals was an important ritual in Roman religious observance. Caesar shows his superstitious nature in Act 2 Scene 2 when he urges the priests to 'do present [immediate] sacrifice' on the morning of his assassination, a ceremony which threatens ill-fortune as the priests 'could not find a heart within the beast'.

Stoics (see p. 126) held to the philosophy of **Stoicism**. It taught that self-control, inner strength and freedom from unsettling emotions were ideal principles that made people indifferent to pleasure and pain and led to clear thinking, balanced judgement and absolute truth. If life became unendurable, it was appropriate to kill yourself.

Suicide was seen as a noble action in the ancient world. The Roman code of honour would dictate that suicide was preferable to ignominious death or disgrace. Brutus vows he will never 'go bound to Rome'; Cassius commits suicide remarking: 'O, coward that I am to live so long'.

◆ Many of the major characters believe their lives are not sacrosanct (see Activity 1 on p. 24). But can suicide ever be a 'noble' act? What do you think Shakespeare's play suggests?

Characters

Julius Caesar

Many historians agree that Caesar was a man of immense talent and great military skill, yet at the same time a mass of contradictions and complexities. This paradoxical mixture of qualities is very much reflected in Shakespeare's portrayal of the most powerful man in the Roman world.

Shakespeare's Caesar dominates the play from the start as the crowd rejoices at his triumph and the tribunes Flavius and Murellus resentfully describe him as the man who intends to 'soar above the view of men'. At the Lupercal ceremony in Act 1 Scene 2 Antony also affirms Caesar's towering authority (line 10): 'When Caesar says, "Do this", it is performed.' Any dissenting voices are ruthlessly silenced (line 275).

Yet Caesar, though powerful, betrays signs of physical weakness and emotional vulnerability. He cannot beget an heir, is deaf in his left ear (a detail that Shakespeare seems to have invented) and suffers from epilepsy. At the very moment when he was publicly being offered a crown we are told how 'He fell down in the market-place, and foamed at mouth, and was speechless' (Act 1 Scene 2, lines 246–7). Cassius also recounts how once he had to rescue Caesar during a swimming contest and how, during a bout of fever, he had cried out 'As a sick girl.'

Yet the same Cassius acknowledges Caesar to 'bestride the narrow world' like a 'Colossus'. Arrogant enough to constantly talk of himself in the third person (as 'Caesar' rather than 'I'), Caesar can at one moment be a shrewd and astute judge of character, warning Antony to be on his guard against Cassius with his 'lean and hungry look', then moments later boast of his own immunity from fear: 'I rather tell thee what is to be feared / Than what I fear: for always I am Caesar' (Act 1 Scene 2, lines 211–12).

Perhaps foolhardy, perhaps fearless, Caesar finally ignores his wife's pleas for him not to go to the Capitol, and in the lead-up to his assassination many of his more unattractive traits are given prominence. Adamantly refusing to repeal the order to banish Metellus' brother, Caesar spurns Metellus 'like a cur [dog]', declaring himself 'constant as the northern star'. This inflexible pride seals his death.

But Caesar's spirit lives on. Antony's moving funeral oration, the blood-drenched corpse, the appearance of his ghost and the fact that both Cassius and Brutus die with Caesar's name on their lips – these all help keep Caesar clearly in the audience's mind to the end of the play.

◆ Which of these two pictures better matches your own impressions of Caesar? Give your reasons.

Brutus

Brutus was a highly educated man from a distinguished family; an ancestor overthrew the tyrannous Tarquin royal family and established the Roman Republic. He fought with Pompey against Caesar, but was pardoned and became Caesar's trusted and close friend. He now sees Caesar as a danger to his Republican idealism.

Perhaps the key to Shakespeare's presentation of him is the sense of conflict that haunts him. By his own admission he is 'Brutus, with himself at war'. In his soliloquy (Act 2 Scene 1, lines 10–34) he reasons very carefully why Caesar must die, concerned to justify all his actions to the highest ethical standard. He believes blindly in the power of rational and logical argument, yet his judgement elsewhere is flawed. He fails to see how Cassius manipulates him, he spares Antony's life, and then lets Antony speak at Caesar's funeral. He heads the conspirators with unquestioned authority, overruling the others on the need to swear an oath, Cicero's suitability as a fellow conspirator and the best way to do battle.

His integrity and reputation are admired by his colleagues. Cassius judges: 'Well, Brutus, thou art noble.' Casca remarks that he 'sits high in all the people's hearts'. To Ligarius he is the 'Soul of Rome'. Brutus himself boasts: 'Set honour in one eye and death i'th'other / And I will look on both indifferently.'

Although these traits lend him a pompous and self-righteous air (perhaps most clearly seen in his quarrel with Cassius in Act 4 Scene 3), his idealism often makes him tragically vulnerable. He has a soft and caring side which surfaces in the domestic scenes where he shows tenderness and concern for his wife Portia and servant Lucius. At the end of the play, even though he is presented as increasingly isolated, he is still seen with the 'remains of friends' who loyally refuse to help him die. Antony's epitaph celebrates powerfully 'the noblest Roman of them all', motivated only by 'common good' rather than 'envy of great Caesar'.

- ◆ In which two scenes do you think the photographs on page 177 were taken? Give your reasons.
- ◆ Write a few paragraphs about the changes and developments in Brutus' character during the course of the play.

Cassius

Cassius fought with Pompey against Caesar and was pardoned, but did not receive Caesar's favour. It is he who drives the initial stages of the conspiracy. Like Brutus he is troubled by the thoughts of what Caesar has become: 'Upon what meat doth this our Caesar feed / That he is grown so great?'

Cassius is prompted by personal resentment and antagonism. These feelings surface powerfully in the way he tries to 'seduce' Brutus to the cause of toppling Caesar. In Act 1 Scene 2 in particular his words seethe with energy and passion as he compares 'we petty men' to the demi-god Caesar. Although Shakespeare does not elaborate on his motives, Cassius expresses his contempt for 'So vile a thing as Caesar' because he 'doth bear me hard' (has a grudge against me). Later in the play (Act 4 Scene 3) Shakespeare suggests that Cassius' temper was inherited from his mother.

Caesar's assessment of Cassius (Act 1 Scene 2) is astute and accurate. Cassius looks predatory and he 'thinks too much'. A shrewd judge of character, he rarely smiles and abjures entertainment. But he is particularly dangerous because such men will forever be restless: 'Whiles they behold a greater than themselves'.

In contrast to Brutus, Cassius has political acumen and cleverness. He knows that the conspiracy will only be successful if all threats are removed (Brutus is obsessed by the need to be 'sacrificers', not 'butchers'). However, he knows that he needs Brutus' support in order to lend their enterprise dignity and nobility and quash any accusations of self-interest on the part of the conspirators.

A key aspect of Cassius' presentation is the change that his character undergoes. He becomes much more sympathetic after the assassination. Like Brutus he attracts loyal followers and shows the deep value of friendship (his reconciliation with Brutus in Act 4 Scene 3 is very moving). Frenzied outbursts give way to calmness. Brutus pays a mournful tribute to him: 'The last of all the Romans'. But perhaps his impetuous suicide capped by Titinius' ironic comment ('thou hast misconstrued everything') is the more appropriate assessment.

♦ Compare the presentation of Cassius in the two images on page 179. Write advice for each Cassius about how to play his difficult role in Act 1.

Antony

Antony was a soldier with a reputation for womanising and riotous living. Shakespeare stresses his virility and social pursuits – he is a Lupercalian runner 'given / To sports, to wildness, and much company'. This reputation endures into Act 5, where Cassius labels him 'a masker and a reveller'. He campaigned with Caesar, reaching high government office through Caesar's favour. Prior to Caesar's assassination he speaks only five lines; in his first appearance he is presented as Caesar's close friend, a man who respects his absolute authority: 'When Caesar says, "Do this", it is performed.' Like that of Brutus, his judgement is seen to be flawed. He mistakenly rates Cassius not dangerous. After Caesar's death Antony really comes into his own. As a deeply grieving friend, master tactician and political opportunist, he holds the stage during the pivotal 'funeral' scene in a mesmerising way.

First he must engage with the murderers. Whilst holding loyally to his love for Caesar, he skilfully negotiates with the assassins, shaking their bloodied hands in an ironic gesture of friendship and respect. But his main objective is to set up his funeral oration to Caesar, and his soliloquy (from Act 3 Scene 1, line 254) shows how false his earlier words have been, the true depth of his grief and the anticipated fury of his revenge.

His funeral speech (from Act 3 Scene 2, line 65), widely regarded as the climactic moment of the play, shows off all Antony's rhetorical skills. Careful not to antagonise the crowd, he first denies he has come to praise Caesar. Dealing with claims about Caesar's ambition, he shows ironic respect for Brutus and sets up memorable choruses and refrains ('honourable man'). The pause to allow the common people to digest his message is a masterstroke. By the time he has re-established Caesar's greatness, planted ideas of mutiny in the minds of the crowd and made reference to the violation of Caesar's cloak, it remains only for him to mention the munificence of Caesar's will and he has unleashed the force of mob violence.

He appears in only four further scenes and is eclipsed by Octavius' cool assurance and control by the end of the play. However, Antony's ruthlessness is underlined by the willing sacrifice of his nephew. He also shows contempt for Lepidus and the integrity of Caesar's will (by siphoning off money to pay for the war against Brutus and Cassius).

At the end of the play, Shakespeare perhaps attempts to recalibrate his presentation of Antony, first by having him pardon Lucilius and secondly by the generosity of his tribute to Brutus in the closing moments.

◆ Which Antony do you think is better suited to the delivery of his funeral oration in Act 3? Give your reasons.

Portia and Calpurnia

These are the only female characters in the play, and they have several features in common. They mirror Elizabethan attitudes to women; they inhabit a world in which men hold complete power and authority and in which women's lives are subservient.

Portia appears in only two scenes. In Act 2 Scene 1 she is used to reveal the impact of Brutus' mental turmoil on his domestic life. She has sensitively and discreetly witnessed the changes in Brutus, but is keen for him to share his burden with her. She makes clear what a loving wife expects 'By all your vows of love' and, in turn, provokes a tender response from Brutus: 'You are my true and honourable wife'. As testament to her love and devotion she has wounded herself in the thigh, a gesture that wrings pity and admiration from her husband. He begs that he might be 'worthy of this noble wife'.

In the scene at the Capitol (Act 2 Scene 4) she displays the gender stereotyping so prevalent in Shakespeare's time, confessing that she finds it hard to keep quiet. It is likely that Brutus has shared the conspirators' plan with her and Portia's natural agitation and nervous anxiety ratchet up the dramatic energy of this episode. Her suicide (by swallowing hot coals) is only reported in Act 4.

'Calpurnia' is the first word that Caesar speaks in the play. Perhaps Shakespeare is drawing attention to Caesar's intimate side as well as reminding the audience that the couple are childless. Later (Act 2 Scene 2) she signals the terrifying portents of the storm and relates a striking dream about her husband's death. In entreating him not to go to the Senate house she provides him with an excuse: 'Call it my fear / That keeps you in the house, and not your own.' Momentarily, Caesar listens, only for Decius to sway the decision by mocking Caesar's adherence to his wife's 'dreams'.

◆ As in Shakespeare's time, this was an all-male production. What challenges does that present to the actor playing Portia?

◆ A tender moment between Calpurnia and Caesar. How far can this be justified from the script?

The language of *Julius Caesar*

Imagery

Some critics have claimed that *Julius Caesar* does not contain much imagery: vivid words and phrases that help create atmosphere as they conjure up emotionally charged pictures or associations in the mind. Yet when Flavius describes the removal of decorations from Caesar's statues, claiming that 'These growing feathers plucked from Caesar's wing / Will make him fly an ordinary pitch' (Act 1 Scene 1, lines 71–2), he is using a striking animal image to compare the limiting of Caesar's power to the way a falconer would restrict the 'pitch' of a falcon (the height to which it rises before swooping) by plucking its feathers. When Flavius adds that Caesar wants to keep his subjects in 'servile [slave-like] fearfulness', the impression of Caesar as a tyrannical predator is complete.

Imagery carries powerful significance. Images enrich particular moments and illuminate key themes. Consider the effect of the following animal images. Caesar dismisses the conspirators' pleas to repeal Metellus' brother's banishment by affirming that he will not respond to 'base spaniel fawning' (behaviour like that of an eager-to-please dog). As Antony contemplates the civil strife that will follow Caesar's murder, he imagines Caesar's ghost will 'Cry havoc and let slip the dogs of war', linking the frenzied mob violence that he has unleashed to the savagery of unruly hounds. In other animal images Caesar is a 'brave hart [deer]' felled by 'hunters' and 'crimsoned in thy Lethe' (Lethe was the river of oblivion in the underworld), or 'like a deer strucken by many princes'.

Other animal images provide insight into character, and intensify meaning and emotional force. When Brutus muses on 'the bright day that brings forth the adder', his train of thought connects hidden danger with the idea of a snake . . . and Caesar. Once Caesar is crowned, 'we put a sting in him / That at his will he may do danger with'. Thus Brutus resolves to 'think him as a serpent's egg . . . And kill him in the shell.'

Shakespeare uses metaphor, simile and personification. All are comparisons which in effect substitute one thing (the image) for another (the thing described).

A **simile** compares one thing to another using 'like' or 'as'. For example, Cassius contemptuously dismisses Caesar dealing with his fever 'As a sick girl'. Caesar 'doth bestride the narrow world / Like a Colossus' (see p. 172). Brutus, contemplating how to execute Caesar rather than slaughter him, implores his fellows to 'carve him as a dish fit for the gods, / Not hew him as a carcass fit for hounds.' Caesar makes his death inevitable by asserting: 'I am constant as the northern star'.

A **metaphor** is also a comparison, suggesting that dissimilar things are the same. Brutus slights Antony, saying he is so dependent on his friend as to be 'but a limb of Caesar'. Urging the conspirators to be 'sacrificers, but not butchers', Brutus shows a high-minded, ethical approach to the killing of Caesar. Portia, aware of an increasingly distant relationship with Brutus, asks: 'Dwell I but in the suburbs / Of your good pleasure?' To Antony the conspirators' 'purpled hands do reek and smoke'.

Personification turns things into persons, giving them human feelings or attributes. Cassius bemoans the state of Rome 'groaning underneath this age's yoke'. Brutus describes 'conspiracy' as like a person ashamed 'to show thy dang'rous brow by night' and celebrates the assassination of Caesar by declaring: 'Ambition's debt is paid.' For Antony, Caesar's bleeding wounds 'like dumb mouths do ope their ruby lips'.

◆ Identify a dozen striking and powerful images in the play. Draw them in a bold, visual way which highlights the comparisons at the heart of each one.

Creating atmosphere

Shakespeare creates atmosphere through language. Choose a favourite scene. Talk together about its atmosphere (aggressive, fearful, joking, and so on). Compile a 'language list' of phrases or lines from your chosen scene which create the atmosphere. Use your list to make up a short play with your own plot and characters. Create as powerful an atmosphere as you can in your play by using Shakespeare's words.

Creating character

Most of Shakespeare's characters have a distinctive way of speaking, but their style can change from situation to situation. For example, Casca's language in Act 1 changes from a relaxed, cynical style in Scene 2 (when he is with his patrician friends) to one of fear and apprehension in the storm of Scene 3.

♦ Choose a character, follow them through the play and compile a list of their 'typical' language in different situations.

Rhetoric

Public speaking (or oratory) was hugely significant in ancient Rome. The art of persuasive speaking and writing, known as 'rhetoric', was a skill that all public figures aspired to master. Scholars developed sophisticated and memorable language techniques that were often used to establish and maintain political power. The art of rhetoric was still considered crucial in Elizabethan times and Shakespeare undoubtedly studied it at school.

Julius Caesar contains many examples of rhetoric: speeches that seek to persuade by using striking and memorable vocabulary and language strategies. Language is used to create atmosphere, persuade people, move them to action, seek to change them. It appeals to their reason, emotions and imagination and builds their confidence in the speaker. In the play rhetoric is used to great effect in several contexts:

- Murellus and Flavius' reprimand of the common people (Act 1 Scene 1)
- Cassius' speeches to Brutus in Act 1 Scene 2
- Brutus in soliloquy where he tries to persuade himself that Caesar's death is justified; Portia's emotional speeches to her husband, imploring him to confide in her (Act 2 Scene 1)
- The Soothsayer's cryptic and ominous warnings to Caesar (Act 2 Scene 4)
- Brutus' speech to the common people, 'Romans, countrymen, and lovers'; Antony's funeral oration, 'Friends, Romans, countrymen' (Act 3 Scene 2)
- Caesar's arrogant assertions of fearlessness (Act 2 Scene 2, Act 3 Scene 1).

Rhetoric uses a range of methods to make language more memorable, in terms of both language selection and its delivery. As well as making extensive use of lists (see p. 187) and repetition (see p. 187), it is very precisely structured and ordered. Key phrases and ideas are reinforced through striking imagery, as in 'Our day is gone, / Clouds, dews, and dangers come' (Act 5 Scene 3, lines 63–4). Listeners are directly engaged through rhetorical questions (ones not requiring an answer) which direct the audience towards the speaker's desired conclusion without the speaker overtly stating it, for example 'Did this in Caesar seem ambitious?' (Act 3 Scene 2, line 82).

◆ Choose one rhetorical speech from the play. Write a short critical evaluation of how it creates its effects, and then record your own interpretation of it.

Antithesis

Antithesis is the opposition of words or phrases to each other, as in 'Set honour in one eye and death i'th'other' (Act 1 Scene 2, line 86); 'honour' and 'death' stand against each other. The setting of word against word is one of Shakespeare's favourite language devices. He uses it extensively in his plays because antithesis powerfully expresses conflict through the use of opposites, and conflict is the essence of drama. Antony remarks of Caesar after his death 'O mighty Caesar! Dost thou lie so low?' Brutus' argument that Antony should not be killed by the conspirators (Act 2 Scene 1, lines 162–83) contains at least a dozen antitheses – 'head' versus 'limbs', 'sacrificers' versus 'butchers' and so on. These antitheses highlight the debate that Brutus is conducting as he tries to present Caesar's assassination as noble rather than brutal and vicious.

◆ Collect more examples of antithesis. Use them in an essay exploring how antithesis creates a sense of conflict in *Julius Caesar*.

Repetition

The repetition that is apparent in the play's language is yet another rhetorical device, used by Shakespeare to create atmosphere, character and dramatic impact. The names 'Caesar' and 'Brutus' each occur over a hundred times in the play. The next most popular words are 'good', 'men' and 'man'. The pattern of repetition reflects some of the play's main concerns: personal identity, the justification and morality of actions, and the appropriate behaviour of men.

◆ On a grander scale, repetition is used in the public speeches. Discuss together how Antony's repeated use of 'honourable' in his funeral oration (Act 3 Scene 2) turns the crowd against the conspirators.

Lists

Another of Shakespeare's favourite language methods is to accumulate words or phrases rather like a list. He intensifies and varies description, atmosphere and argument as he 'piles up' item on item, incident on incident. Brutus uses lists in his funeral oration addressed to the people of Rome (Act 3 Scene 2, lines 13–39): 'There is tears for his love, joy for his fortune, honour for his valour, / and death for his ambition.' Antony likewise lists 'all thy conquests, glories, triumphs, spoils' (Act 3 Scene 1, line 149), and towards the end of his funeral oration (Act 3 Scene 2, lines 211–13) ironically suggests that as a speaker he has 'neither wit, nor words, nor worth, / Action, nor utterance, nor the power of speech / To stir men's blood.'

◆ Lists also help to accentuate the details of the storm (Act 1 Scene 3, lines 59–78) and Calpurnia's description of the omens seen by the guards (Act 2 Scene 2, lines 13–24). Discuss together the effects created by these lists.

Verse and prose

How did Shakespeare decide whether to write in verse or prose? One answer is that he followed theatrical convention. Prose was tradition-ally used by comic and low-status characters. High-status characters spoke verse. Comic scenes were written in prose (as were letters), but audiences expected verse in the serious scenes: the poetic style was thought to be particularly suitable for moments of high dramatic or emotional intensity, and for tragic themes.

The Commoners (low-status characters) speak in prose in the first scene although Flavius and Murellus (high status) use verse. How-ever, during Caesar's funeral individual members of the crowd speak in verse, perhaps to underline the emotional intensity of the scene. Another remarkable departure from this prose or verse convention is Brutus' funeral oration (Act 3 Scene 2) which is in prose, although Brutus' language here clearly demonstrates that Shakespeare can use prose just as effectively as verse to express the deepest feelings and the most profound thoughts.

With few other exceptions, the verse of *Julius Caesar* is blank verse: unrhymed verse written in iambic pentameter. Shakespeare would probably have learned the technical definition of iambic penta-meter at school. In Greek *penta* means 'five' and an *iamb* is a 'foot' (or group) of two syllables, the first unstressed and the second stressed, as in the pronunciation of 'alas': a LAS. Iambic pentameter is therefore metrical verse in which each line has five stressed syllables (/) altern-ating with five unstressed syllables (×), as in this line by Cassius:

× /　　× /　×　 /　×　/　×　 /
I know where I will wear this dagger then

- Read the line aloud in unison with your partner, pronouncing each syllable very clearly, almost as if each were a separate word. As you read beat out the five-stress rhythm (e.g. clap hands, tap the desk).
- Now turn to the closing eight lines of Act 1 Scene 3. Repeat what you have just done. Can you find the rhythm? When you have found it, try the exercise again with verse spoken by other characters.

By the time Shakespeare wrote *Julius Caesar*, he was becoming more flexible and experimental in his use of iambic pentameter. **End-stopped** lines (lines with a pause at the end) are less frequent and there is a greater use of **enjambement** (where one line flows into the next).

- Find examples of both end-stopping and enjambement in Brutus' speech (Act 2 Scene 1, lines 162–83). Describe the different effects Shakespeare creates using these metrical techniques.

Julius Caesar in performance

Julius Caesar was probably first performed in 1599 and seems to have been a popular play from the start. It was almost certainly one of the earliest productions by Shakespeare's own company at their newly built Globe Theatre. There were no elaborate sets on Shakespeare's Globe stage. Plays were performed in broad daylight and in the open air, so that to create the night-time storm scene of Act 1 Scene 3 Shakespeare needed to rely heavily on the power of his language to evoke the right atmosphere.

Caesar (left) with Brutus in the 400th anniversary production (1999) at the new Globe Theatre in London. Describe your impressions of the authentic Elizabethan stage and costumes.

Reflecting the practice of Shakespeare's time, all the parts in the 1999 new Globe production, including the women, were played by men. Most of the principal actors wore lavish Elizabethan costume (like the ones above), but some of the minor characters, such as the Plebeians and the Soothsayer, mingled with the audience dressed in modern clothes like jeans and baseball caps. This continued a trend seen in recent productions to involve the audience directly as the crowd in the public scenes, thus giving the play a more contemporary resonance.

During the seventeenth and eighteenth centuries Shakespeare's script was often modified to suggest more strongly that Brutus was the central character and thereby heighten his tragic status. He was for example given a more impressive death scene in one production, where he was allowed to kill himself without the aid of Strato. There was also a trend to scale down the importance of the 'supernatural' elements.

In the nineteenth century some productions focused on the re-creation of the splendid setting of Rome with lavish scenery and costume. The architecture was carefully designed and the 'public' elements such as the lavish processions and crowd scenes were hand-somely staged. The text continued to be adjusted to showcase Brutus as a noble and patriotic hero and Antony as a high-minded avenger. This meant that some of the play had to be cut (e.g. Antony's ruthless political activity in Act 4 Scene 1) because it jarred with the overall tone of the production.

William Charles Macready, staging the play in the early 1800s, gave the crowd scenes greater dramatic prominence, which set the trend for late nineteenth-century versions in which the forum scene (and Antony) were seen as central to the play. Herbert Beerbohm Tree's production in 1898 also emphasised the active involvement of the crowd and highlighted the way in which Antony manipulated the crowd, so that he now became the leading figure in the play. There was also an attempt to instil greater complexity and richness into the presentation of Caesar. Tree's commitment to visual spec-tacle produced a series of 'Roman daily life' scenes which he inserted before Shakespeare's opening scene in order to establish a Roman context.

The twentieth century saw a return to much simpler stagings of the play. There was still some extravagance, but the dependence on theatrical illusion disappeared and productions concentrated on the clarity of the language. Just as Shakespeare probably intended, scenes flowed swiftly into each other and the action was not held up by clumsy stagecraft. Orson Welles' landmark 1937 production was subtitled *Death of a Dictator* and was heavily focused on the play's political elements. The 1955 film resonated with references to Mussolini and Hitler.

In the last decades of the twentieth century many productions tried to link the play with contemporary events. Julius Caesar was played as Latin American dictator, resembled Egypt's assassinated President Sadat and identified with the freedom fighter Che Guevara. Rome was used to symbolise Germany in the 1930s and East European dictator-ships. In the last of these interpretations, Caesar was followed con-tinually by a secret policeman and TV camera and the actors moved amongst the audience, who found themselves playing the part of the Roman citizens.

Short reviews of more recent productions

- The 1995 RSC production was cut to two hours' running time. An 8-foot marble head of Caesar dominated the beginning and ending (see p. 193), and there was a huge amount of visual imagery – buckets of blood, red togas and a blood–red crack through Caesar's image in the storm scene. It was a production that emphasised the symbolism of the play.

- In 2001 the RSC again stressed the play's political dimensions, this time by creating a set that resembled the Nazi Nuremberg rallies (see p. 179, top). The fascist references were echoed by the wearing of ceremonial togas combined with jackboots and black shirts.

- The RSC took their 2004 production on tour, using improvised and unconventional venues (see p. 139). The rawness and tough-ness of the set, reminiscent of industrial Eastern Europe, attracted a young audience. The Roman mob was dressed in fashionable casual clothes, while the soundtrack and lighting were sinisterly threaten-ing.

- The 2005 Barbican production deployed a hundred extras, which gave the mob tremendous energy and power (see pp. 5, 80). Very much a modern–dress version, it opened like a movie premiere based around cool, slick marble and glass. For the battle scenes the fighters wore American–style battle dress and helmets and the set was like a vast, devastated warehouse.

- The 2006 RSC production (see pp. 14, 39) used a minimalist set, just a gravel area surrounded by a pitch–black void. The storm scene was very dramatic, using real rain and crackling electricity. The senators wore predominantly red outfits under crisp white togas.

- Choose one or more ideas from the above production reviews which you find interesting and describe in detail what special qualities you think they added to those productions.

♦ Some critics feel that setting *Julius Caesar* in a different historical or political period from ancient Rome causes problems for a modern audience. What do you think?

♦ Talk together about the staging opportunities offered by the set shown below and the one on page 194. What do you think the set designers had in mind?

Stage your own production of *Julius Caesar*

Talk together about the period and place in which you will set your production. Clearly any historical setting other than a Roman one could have wider political resonances. Then choose one or more of the following activities:

- Design the basic set. If your production is going to be school-based, you will need to work with a particular space in mind (either indoors or outdoors). Decide where you want the audience to be seated. Consider whether you want a thrust stage or to present your play 'in the round' or as a promenade performance. Sketch your set or make a three-dimensional model of it. Work out how you will depict the domestic scenes (inside Brutus' and Caesar's homes), the Capitol scenes and the battles.
- Design the costumes. Study some of the ways Caesar and the conspirators have been presented. Think about how you will dress Portia and Calpurnia to reflect their roles and relationships with their husbands. How will you dress the common people?
- Design the props. Three important ones are Cassius' sword (see p. 154), Pompey's statue and Caesar's battle cloak.
- Design a sound effects programme to accompany any one scene.
- Design a publicity poster. Use illustrations and language that will make people take notice.

◆ Design the programme. It could include a summary of the plot, a cast list, interviews with the actors, a history of recent productions and rehearsal photographs.

◆ Cast the play. Suggest people at your school or college, or from the world of television, theatre or the media.

◆ Choose any scene from the play and produce your version of a director's prompt book for it. Your prompt book should include detailed notes about the ways in which you want the actors to perform the script, notes on the setting and props, on entrances and exits – anything to help you to bring that scene to life.

William Shakespeare
1564–1616

1564 Born Stratford-upon-Avon, eldest son of John and Mary Shakespeare.

1582 Marries Anne Hathaway of Shottery, near Stratford.

1583 Daughter, Susanna, born.

1585 Twins, son and daughter, Hamnet and Judith, born.

1592 First mention of Shakespeare in London. Robert Greene, another playwright, described Shakespeare as 'an upstart crow beautified with our feathers . . .'. Greene seems to have been jealous of Shakespeare. He mocked Shakespeare's name, calling him 'the only Shake-scene in a country' (presumably because Shakespeare was writing successful plays).

1595 A shareholder in The Lord Chamberlain's Men, an acting company that became extremely popular.

1596 Son Hamnet dies, aged eleven.
       Father, John, granted arms (acknowledged as a gentleman).

1597 Buys New Place, the grandest house in Stratford.

1598 Acts in Ben Jonson's *Every Man in His Humour*.

1599 Globe Theatre opens on Bankside. Performances in the open air.

1601 Father, John, dies.

1603 James I grants Shakespeare's company a royal patent: The Lord Chamberlain's Men become The King's Men and play about twelve performances each year at court.

1607 Daughter, Susanna, marries Dr John Hall.

1608 Mother, Mary, dies.

1609 The King's Men begin performing indoors at Blackfriars Theatre.

1610 Probably returns from London to live in Stratford.

1616 Daughter, Judith, marries Thomas Quiney.
       Dies. Buried in Holy Trinity Church, Stratford-upon-Avon.

The plays and poems
(no one knows exactly when he wrote each play)

1589–95 *The Two Gentlemen of Verona, The Taming of the Shrew, First, Second and Third Parts of King Henry VI, Titus Andronicus, King Richard III, The Comedy of Errors, Love's Labour's Lost, A Midsummer Night's Dream, Romeo and Juliet, King Richard II* (and the long poems *Venus and Adonis* and *The Rape of Lucrece*).

1596–9 *King John, The Merchant of Venice, First and Second Parts of King Henry IV, The Merry Wives of Windsor, Much Ado About Nothing, King Henry V, Julius Caesar* (and probably the *Sonnets*).

1600–5 *As You Like It, Hamlet, Twelfth Night, Troilus and Cressida, Measure for Measure, Othello, All's Well That Ends Well, Timon of Athens, King Lear.*

1606–11 *Macbeth, Antony and Cleopatra, Pericles, Coriolanus, The Winter's Tale, Cymbeline, The Tempest.*

1613 *King Henry VIII, The Two Noble Kinsmen* (both probably with John Fletcher).

1623 Shakespeare's plays published as a collection (now called the First Folio).